BRAIN BOGGLING PUZZLES FOR SMART KIDS

101+ LOGIC PUZZLES, WORD GAMES, BRAIN TEASERS, AND MORE!

FOR AGES 8 AND UP

Produced by Beaky and Starlight Ltd.

Published : October 2021

ISBN: 9798754213760 (Hardback), 9798491917044 (Paperback)

For more information about the publisher, please visit:

www.facebook.com/BeakyAndStarlight/

THIS BOOK BELONGS TO

____

Puzzle 1

Treasure Map

Hidden by a legendary pirate, a chest of treasures is waiting to be discovered on this island. Find out the missing letters in the word puzzles below and cross out the corresponding row or column on the map. The map square left open is where the treasure is!

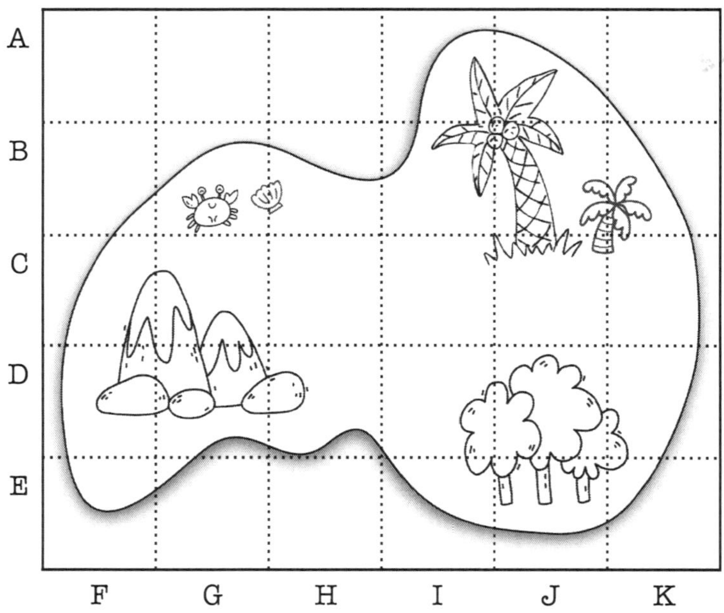

PIR_TE

C_EST

_RAB

_LA_

HOO_

F_SH

_OTTLE

_AGGER

Pirate Word Search

Ahoy! Can you find all these pirate words? They might be written horizontally or vertically, and either forwards or backwards.

BEACH
CAPTAIN
GOLD
LAND
MAP
SHIP
SAILOR
PARROT
CAVE
LEGEND

P	N	H	G	E	H	C	A	E	B
I	S	A	O	Z	H	O	V	P	I
H	A	I	L	H	E	F	V	D	O
S	I	D	D	S	V	A	C	M	I
P	L	Z	C	U	A	C	A	A	P
P	O	A	D	T	C	I	P	P	A
H	R	S	D	K	F	S	T	P	R
L	E	G	E	N	D	P	A	M	R
Z	P	M	K	B	H	L	I	S	O
Y	L	A	N	D	E	E	N	N	T

Puzzle 3

Spot the difference

Spot ten differences between these two pictures.

4x4 Sudoku

Put numbers in the empty squares so that every row, column, and box with thicker lines includes the numbers 1, 2, 3, and 4.

A

3			4
2	4		
			2
4		3	1

B

4	3		1
		4	3
1			2
	2		

C

4			2
	3	1	4
1		2	
			1

D

			4
2		1	3
1			2
	2		1

Puzzle 5

What's Next?

What comes next in each sequence below?

A

B

C

D

Message in a Bottle

A bottle with a message has been found. Can you read the message and use the map to locate the desert island?

Hi, my name is Louis Roberts. I'm stranded on an island. I was sailing from Mango Island to Coconut Island when a hurricane destroyed my boat.

The island I'm on has a sandy beach on one side and a cliff on the other side. When standing on the beach I can see some other islands, but looking out from the cliff I can't see any other island. There is no building on this island, so I built a shelter using palm leaves. I also collect rainwater with palm leaves as there's no river.

It's peaceful here, but I miss my family and having a hot cup of tea. Please help.

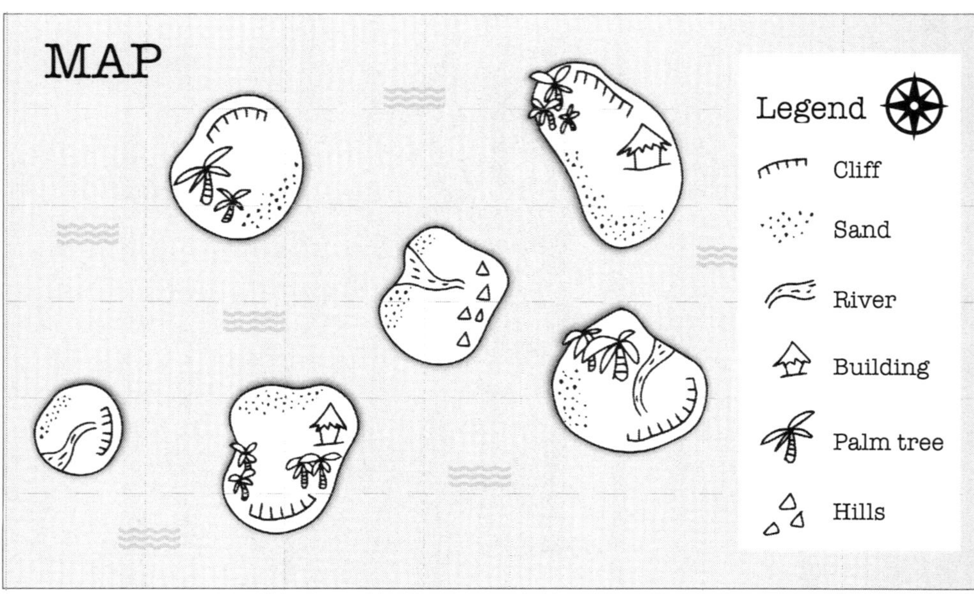

Puzzle 8

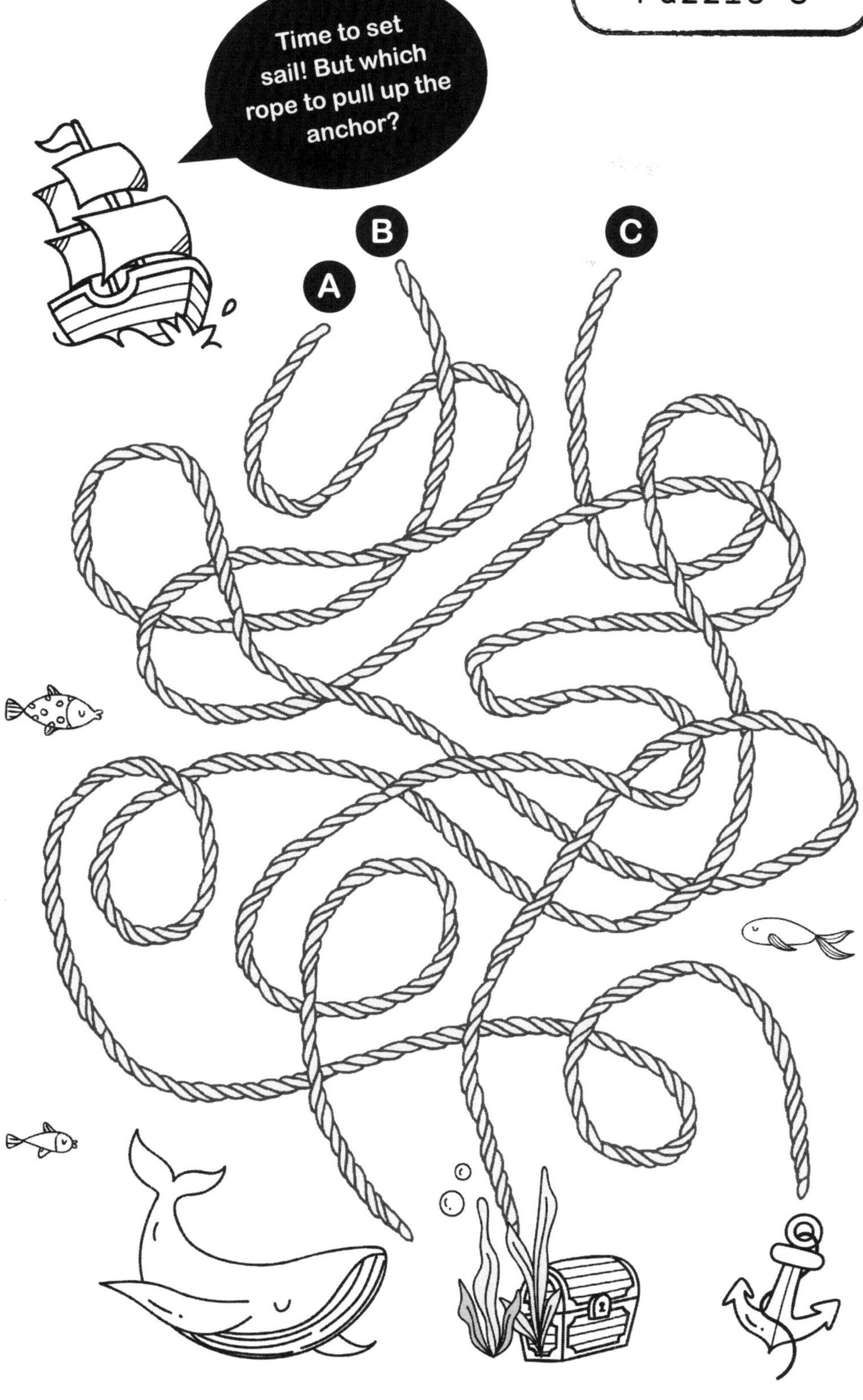

Puzzle 9

Divide it!

Can you divide the picture below into four sections using two straight lines? Each section must include all five different items.

Missing Numbers

The grids below are missing some numbers. Can you put numbers 1,2,3,4, or 5 in the empty squares so that every row and every column in both grids contain all five numbers.

A

1	2	3	4	5
		5		2
			2	
		2		3
2		1	5	4

B

5		2		4
	4		3	
2		3		5
	5		2	
3		4		1

Puzzle 11

Picture Crossword

Fill our names into the grid to complete the crossword puzzle!

ACROSS

1.

5.

6.

8.

10.

DOWN

2.

3.

4.

7.

9.

Tracing Lines

Start from the dotted circle, and trace the lines of each shape without going over any of the lines twice, or taking your pen off. One of the shapes below is impossible to trace without going over a line twice. Can you identify it?

A

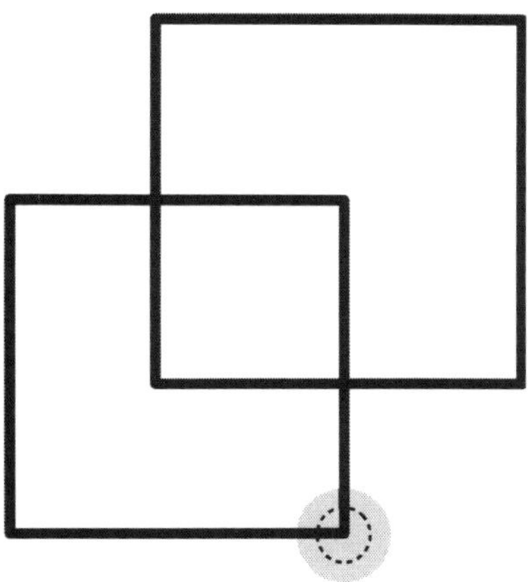

B

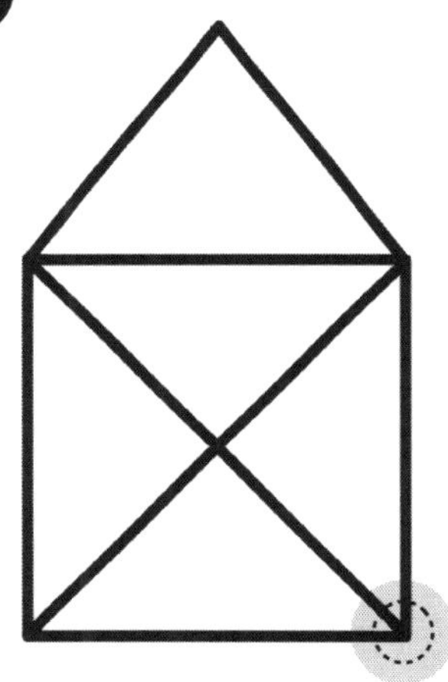

C

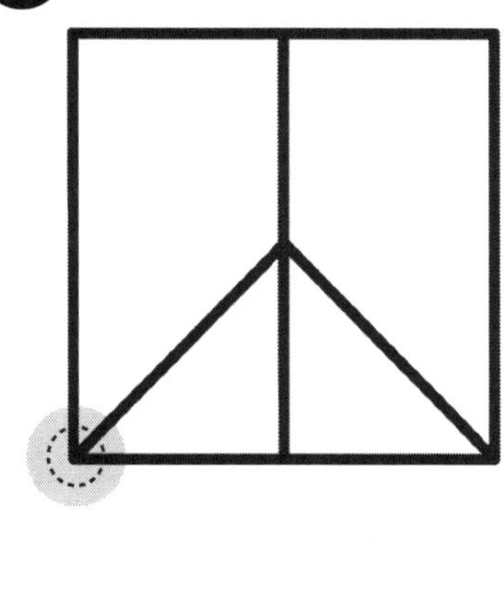

D

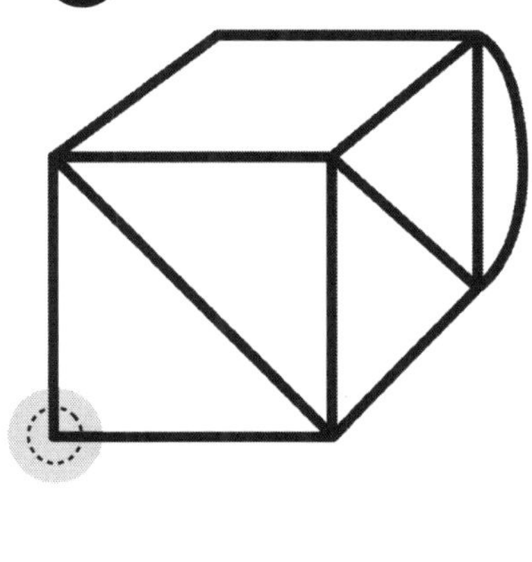

Puzzle 13

Futoshiki Puzzle

Fill in numbers in the empty squares so that every row and column includes the numbers 1, 2, 3, and 4. Use the inequality signs as clues and make sure the numbers obey the inequality sign between them. This means, the pointy arrow between two numbers always points at the smaller one.

Example 1

3	<	

On the first row of the puzzle, you will find the above squares. This means the missing number here is greater than 3. We know that the only number that is between 1 to 4 and greater than 3 is 4. Therefore the missing number is 4.

Example 2

A	<	3
V		
B		

On the third and fourth rows of the puzzle, you will find these squares. This means the missing number A is less than 3 and greater than the missing number B. We know the numbers that are between 1 to 4 and less than 3 are 1 and 2. Therefore A and B can only be 1 or 2, and for A to be greater than B, A must be 2 and B must be 1.

3	<	4				2
		V				
		2	<	3		
		V		V		
		1			<	3

Lying Pirate

You've captured a pirate and his three treasure chests. However not all treasure chests contain gold and silver, instead, there are snakes and scorpions. The cheeky pirate gave three statements and you know he never tells the truth. Can you figure out which chests hold real treasure?

Puzzle 15

Broken Words

Someone has torn a list of school supplies into pieces. Could you figure out what was on the list? You can find clues from pictures on this page.

rul scis

cra ck

book glo

clo er

note ue

yon cil

uter sharp

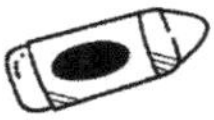

comp sors gl

ener be

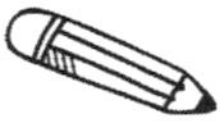

pen

1 ______________________ 6 ______________________

2 ______________________ 7 ______________________

3 ______________________ 8 ______________________

4 ______________________ 9 ______________________

5 ______________________ 10 ______________________

Fun Maths

Maths is great fun, but the equations below are wrong. Can you move one pencil in each equation to make them correct?

A

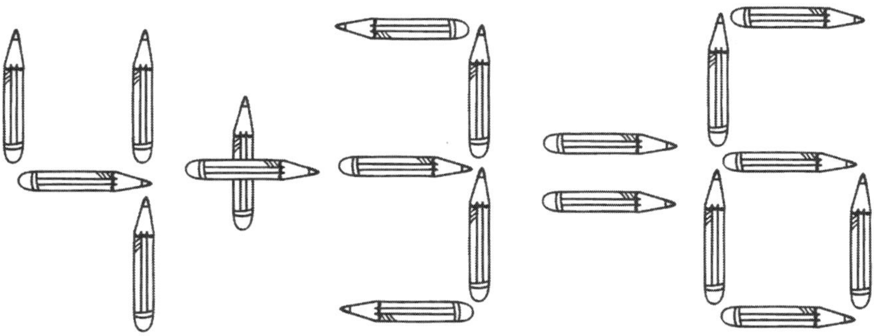

B

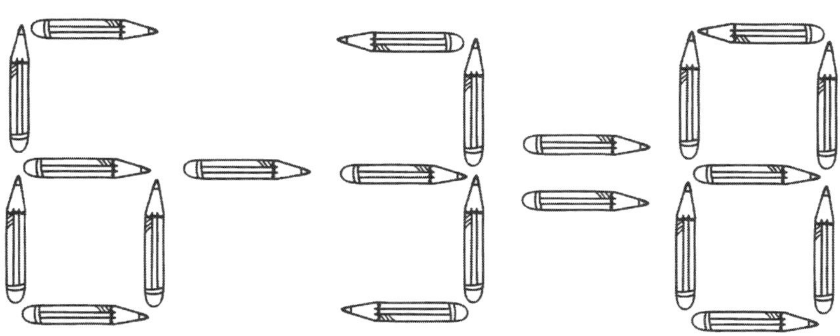

Puzzle 17

Dr. Seuss Word Snake

What did Dr. Seuss write about learning in *I can read with my eyes shut*?

Start from the triangle and finish with the dot, find words one by one and rebuild the sentence. Remember you can move up, down, or sideways but not diagonally.

▶ T	H	E	M	O	R	E
E	R	O	M	T	N	T
P	O	U	E	H	R	H
L	Y	W	L	E	A	A
A	S	I	U	O	Y	T
C	E	L	L	G	O	●

Write it down here

____

____

Finding Pairs

Find 5 pairs of identical items in the picture below.

Puzzle 19

Crossword

Use the clues to solve this puzzle. All words in this crossword are school subjects.

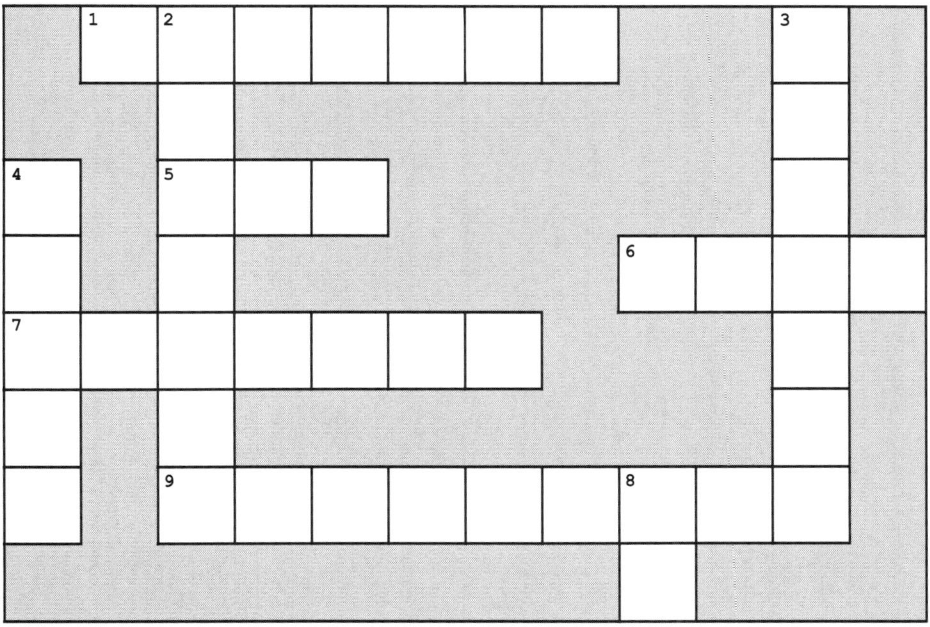

DOWN

2 Learning to understand written words

3 Study of what happened in the past

4 Study of melody and instruments

8 Sport and physical activity

ACROSS

1 Study to create written work

5 Paintings, drawings, and sculptures

6 Study of numbers, shapes, and space

7 Study of the world through observation and experimentation

9 Study of the Earth's surface

Domino Puzzle

Can you place these domino pieces in the grey spaces below to complete the domino chain? Each domino has two halves, only the halves with the same number can touch each other.

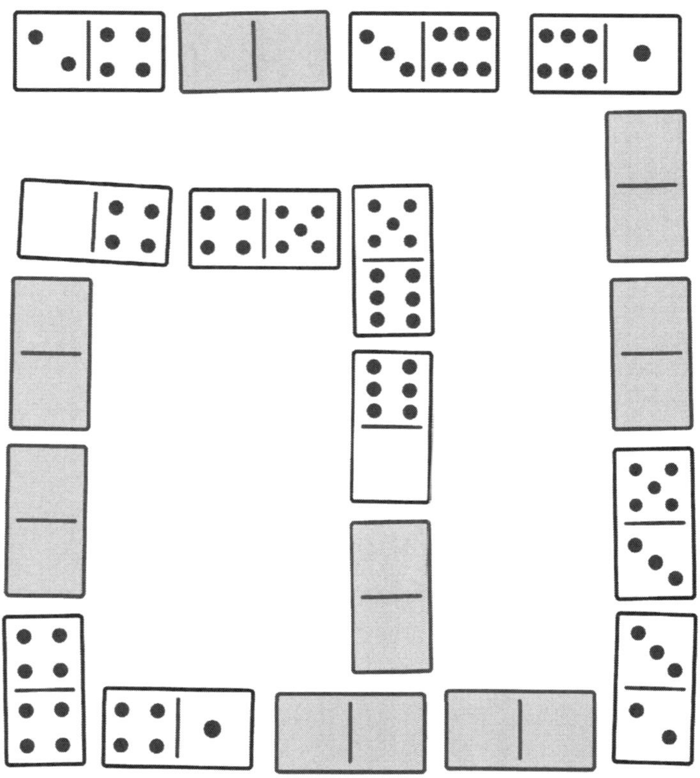

Sports Day Mystery

Sports day is coming but a few very important pieces of equipment have been hidden by some cheeky students. They left a note with some secret codes. To decode the message, look up the numbers in the code-cracker, choose one of the two letters, and form a word. For example: 10, 8, 13 = S~~T~~, ~~O~~P, Y~~Z~~ = SPY.

Head to the 1, 9, 10 room for the trophy.

Find the medals in the garden 10, 4, 3, 2.

The stop watch is hidden in the 4, 13, 7.

The whistles are in the 7, 11, 10, 5, 2 room.

Code-cracker

1 = AB	8 = OP
2 = CD	9 = QR
3 = EF	10 = ST
4 = GH	11 = UV
5 = IJ	12 = WX
6 = KL	13 = YZ
7 = MN	

____

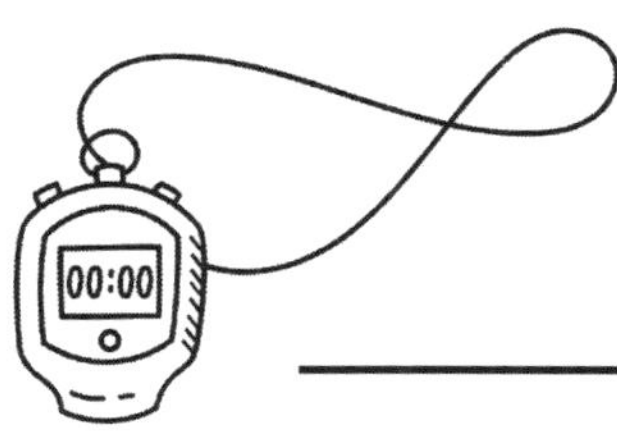

____

____

____

Puzzle 23

Number Triangle

In these triangles, the numbers in the square boxes are the sum of the two numbers in connected circles. For example:

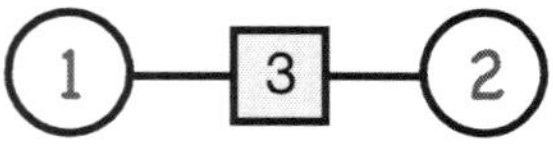

Can you figure out which number should be in each of the circles? They are between 1 to 9 and can only be used once in each triangle.

A

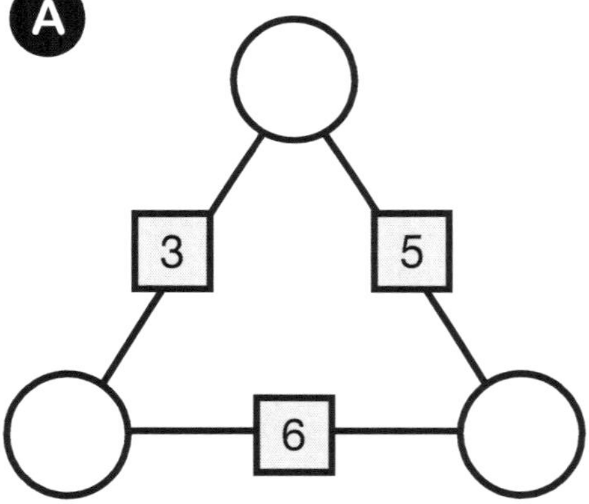

B

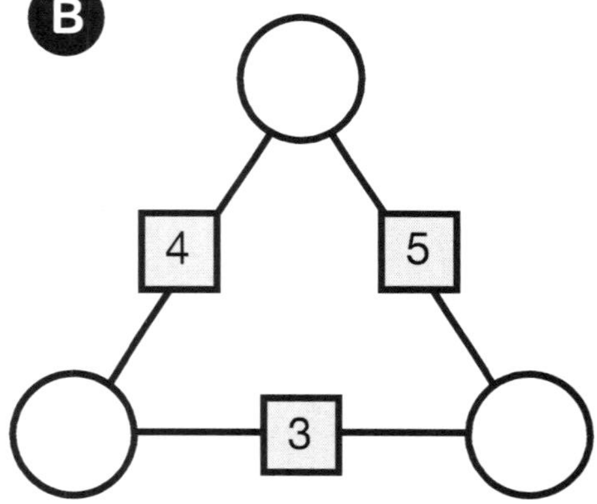

C

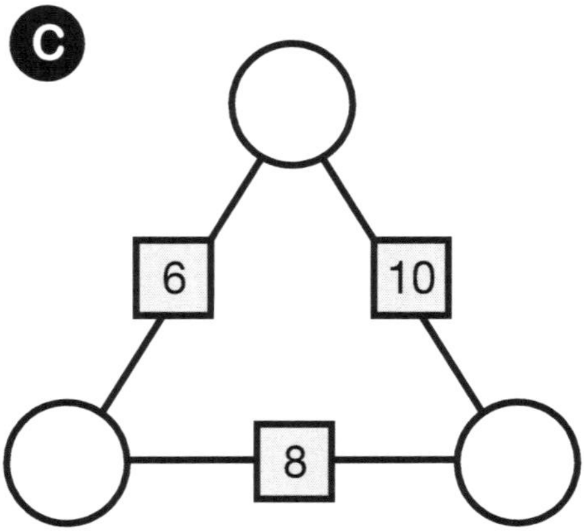

D

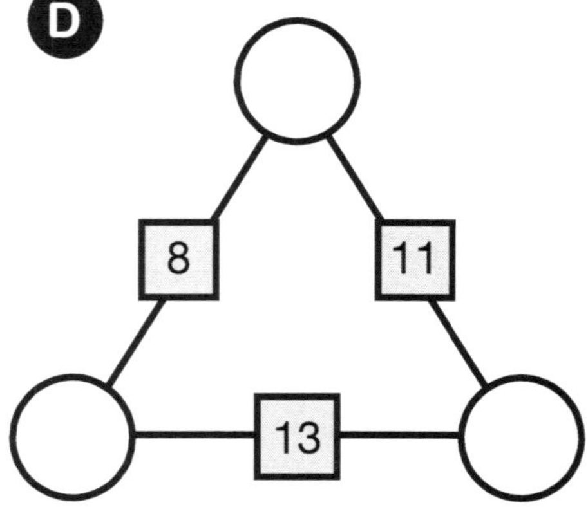

Puzzle 24

Word Search

Can you find all these school items in the word search puzzle below? They might be written horizontally or vertically, and either forwards or backwards.

BOOK	POSTER	PAPER
DESK	FOLDER	TAPE
ATLAS	MARKER	EASEL

T W E G E A T L A S
A S P A P E R V O I
P Q R L H E F V P J
E G R D T V R C O H
D L T C Y Y E A S M
K O O B T N D U T W
H R R D D F L T E K
L E S A E D O A R S
A F S S A S F H H E
M A R K E R G N N D

Puzzle 25

6x6 Sudoku

Place numbers in the empty squares so that every row, column, and box with thicker lines includes the numbers 1, 2, 3, 4, 5, and 6.

A

5	2				
6		4		2	
1	4	6		5	2
					6
2		3		1	5
		5	2	6	

B

		4	2		
2		5	3	1	
	4				1
		1	6		
		3		5	
1	5		4	2	

Age Puzzle

Four children are comparing their age and all of them are telling the truth. Can you figure out who is the oldest and who is the youngest?

Kyudoku Puzzle

Select numbers 1 to 9 in the grid so that in each row and column the sum of the selected numbers adds up to 9 or less. Each number can only be selected once.

2	4	1	**(6)**	3	9
3	6	6	9	1	9
2	8	7	2	8	7
8	7	6	4	2	9
1	4	6	8	5	5
7	8	**(1)**	8	7	5

Tips:

1. In the puzzle above, the correct 1 and 6 have been found so all other 1s and 6s in the grid can be crossed out as they no longer can be part of the solution.
2. Eliminate those numbers that would make a column or row to add up to more than 9.
3. If there is a number that appears only once in the grid, it must be the correct one.

Which animal?

This mysterious animal lives in the icy water of the Arctic sea. It has two teeth, but usually only one develops. It can dive about a mile deep in the ocean and feeds on fish, squid, and shrimp.

To find out what animal it is, solve the puzzles with the clues below and read the answer in the highlighted column.

Clues:

1 Cheeky animal with a long tail

2 Animal that has kids and a beard

3 Stripy horse that's from Africa

4 Nighttime bird of prey

5 Largest land animal

6 Animal that loves eating bamboo

7 Smart sea mammal that loves to play

Puzzle 29

Spot the difference

Find the 10 differences between these two pictures.

Animal characters

There are many animal characters in the classic story of *Alice's Adventures in Wonderland*. Four of them are hidden in the letter grid below. Draw a circle around every fifth letter and find out who they are.

G	B	B	V	D	F	Z	J	B	O	Z	F	N	T	R	F
B	S	T	M	W	T	D	U	O	D	E	N	J	U	G	N
G	X	S	Z	C	N	J	E	M	C	X	G	C	Q	O	G
F	H	C	Y	T	J	E	D	O	Q	H	S	Y	J	M	U
H	B	T	Q	W	I	V	H	D	H	R	C	H	M	Y	E
F	R	V	B	C	O	S	J	Y	A	Y	N	F	S	T	N
X	A	L	C	S	F	W	R	A	E	H	P	E	T	P	P
Y	S	E	A	M	X	S	R	F	S	X	N	P	F	E	N
P	I	I	T	J	Q	L	X	N	P	O	L	Z	V	P	Z
A	M	X	G	E	R	X	J	V	J	W	D	O	O	P	H
C	H	C	S	I	J	Q	W	O	T	F	P	L	F	E	P
B	Q	W	R	P	W	Q	I	A	H	Y	E	F	B	X	E
X	E	B	W	Q	D	H	I	A	V	K	N	T	R	Q	N

Puzzle 31

12 Animals

In the Chinese zodiac, every year is associated with an animal. It cycles every 12 years, starting with the year of the Rat and ending with the year of the Pig.

Reading the clues given by this family and checking out the year chart, can you figure out which year and animal each of them was born in?

Rat	2020	2008	1996	1984	1972
Ox	2021	2009	1997	1985	1973
Tiger	2022	2010	1998	1986	1974
Rabbit	2023	2011	1999	1987	1975
Dragon	2024	2012	2000	1988	1976
Snake	2025	2013	2001	1989	1977
Horse	2026	2014	2002	1990	1978
Goat	2027	2015	2003	1991	1979
Monkey	2028	2016	2004	1992	1980
Rooster	2029	2017	2005	1993	1981
Dog	2030	2018	2006	1994	1982
Pig	2031	2019	2007	1995	1983

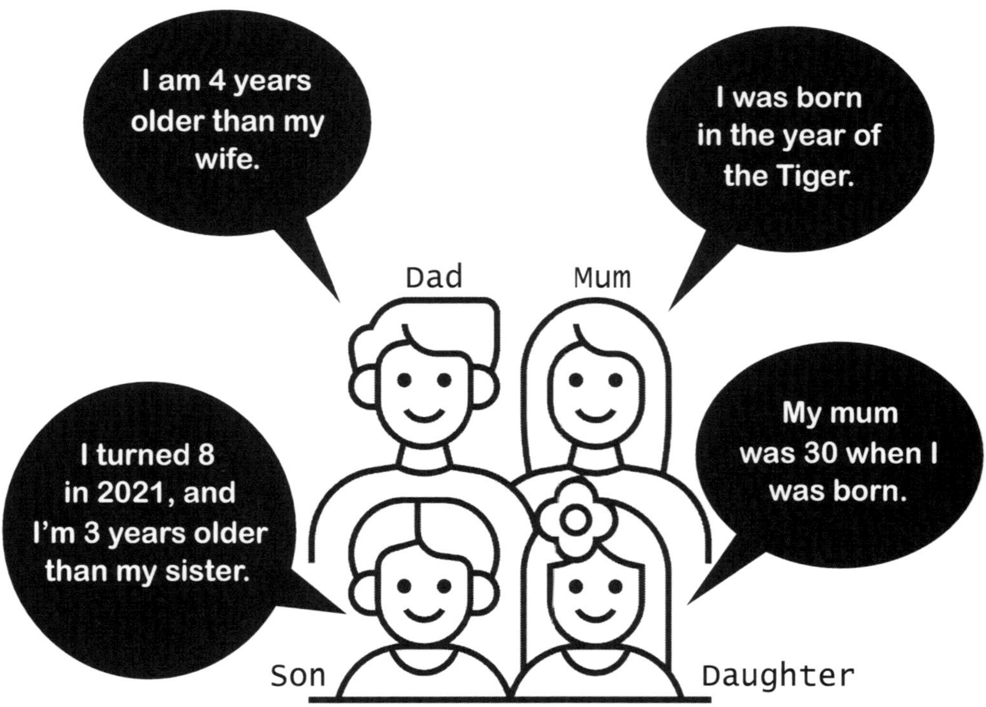

Number Pyramid

In this pyramid, the number in each square is the sum of the two numbers below it. Can you fill in all the empty squares?

137					
		15			
	11			13	
	9		3		6

Puzzle 33

Nocturnal Crossword

Can you solve the clues to complete this puzzle? All words are a nocturnal animal.

DOWN

1 Mammal that hangs upside down when sleeping

4 Big cat that lives in prides

5 Dam-building animal

7 Cute spiny mammal

8 Clothes-eating insect

ACROSS

2 Big cat with yellow coat and black stripes

3 Hooting bird of prey

5 Mammal with black-and-white striped face

6 Tunnel-digging mammal

9 Small and timid rodent

11 Sly animal with bushy tail

Messy Zoo

The zookeeper needs help to place all these animals in the right area. Can you draw three straight lines to divide the zoo into four areas so similar animals stay together?

Puzzle 35

Bridge Puzzle

Draw lines between islands so the number of lines connected to each island matches the number on the island.

Rules:

a. The bridges must be straight lines without bends

b. The bridges can not intersect with each other

c. The bridges can be horizontal or vertical but not diagonal

d. The maximum number of bridges between two islands is 2

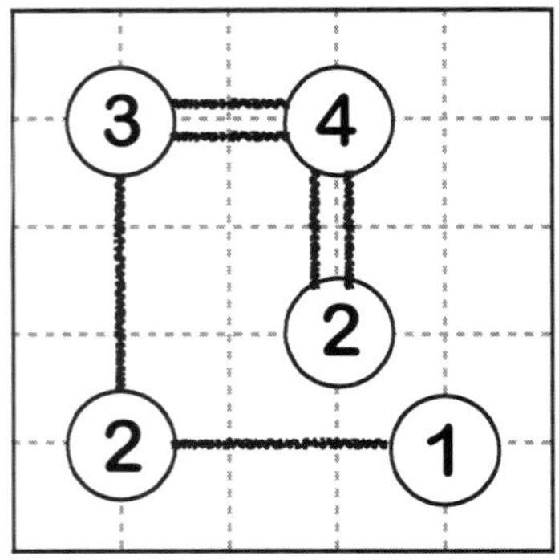

THIS EXAMPLE SHOWS HOW IT WORKS

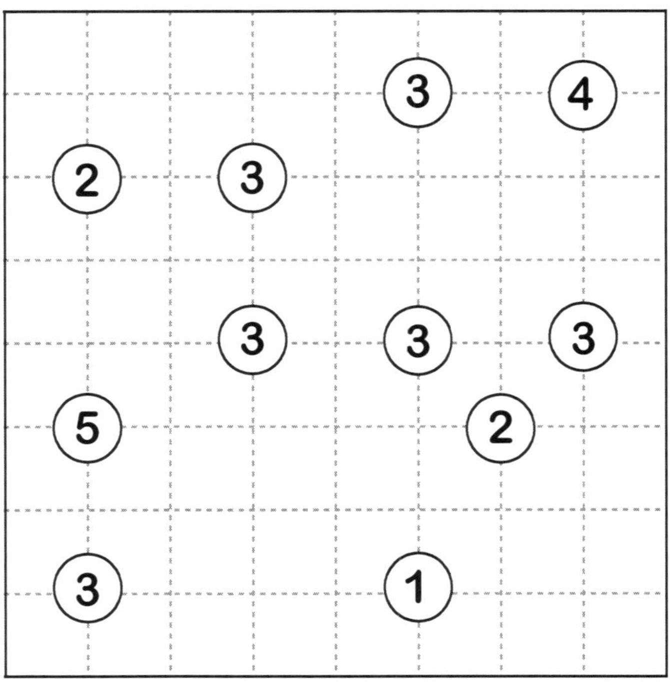

Animal Footprints

Can you find out which animal each of these footprints belongs to?

Puzzle 37

Hello! I am a combination of 10 animals. Can you figure out what they are?

Arrow Words

Could you solve this word puzzle? The clues are in the grey squares, and the arrows from the clue point to the squares where the answer words should go. All the words go from left to right, or top to bottom, no matter which direction the arrow points. Some clues are pictures!

Afternoon	B	A	T	H	
		School gym class		How old you are	Fail to win
Type of animal that produces milk		A long time ___			
The "S" in U.S.A.		___ and the Beast			

Nonograms

Your goal in these puzzles is to find the black squares in the grid and fill them in. The numbers on the top of each column tell you the lengths of continuous black squares in that column, and the numbers on the left of each row are the indications for the lengths of continuous black squares in that row.

CHECK OUT THIS EXAMPLE

TOP TIPS:

a. Use a pencil so it's easier to make marks and changes

b. Start with the numbers that are equal to the size of the row or column

c. Repeatedly check each clue and mark those squares that you're certain should stay white with a dot or cross

d. If there is a 0 in the clues, make sure the whole row or column stays white

A

	1	3	5	3	1
1					
3					
5					
3					
1					

B

	1	5	0	1 3	1 1 1	3 1	0	1 1	1 1 1	5
2 3 3										
1 1 1										
1 3 2										
1 1 1										
1 3 3										

START HERE AND FIND YOUR WAY OUT!

Multiplication Tree

In the multiplication tree, the numbers in the circles are the multiplication product of the two numbers that are connected below. The bottom row of this tree contains the numbers 1 to 6, each only appears once. Could you figure out the rest of the numbers in the tree?

A CALCULATOR MIGHT BE HANDY

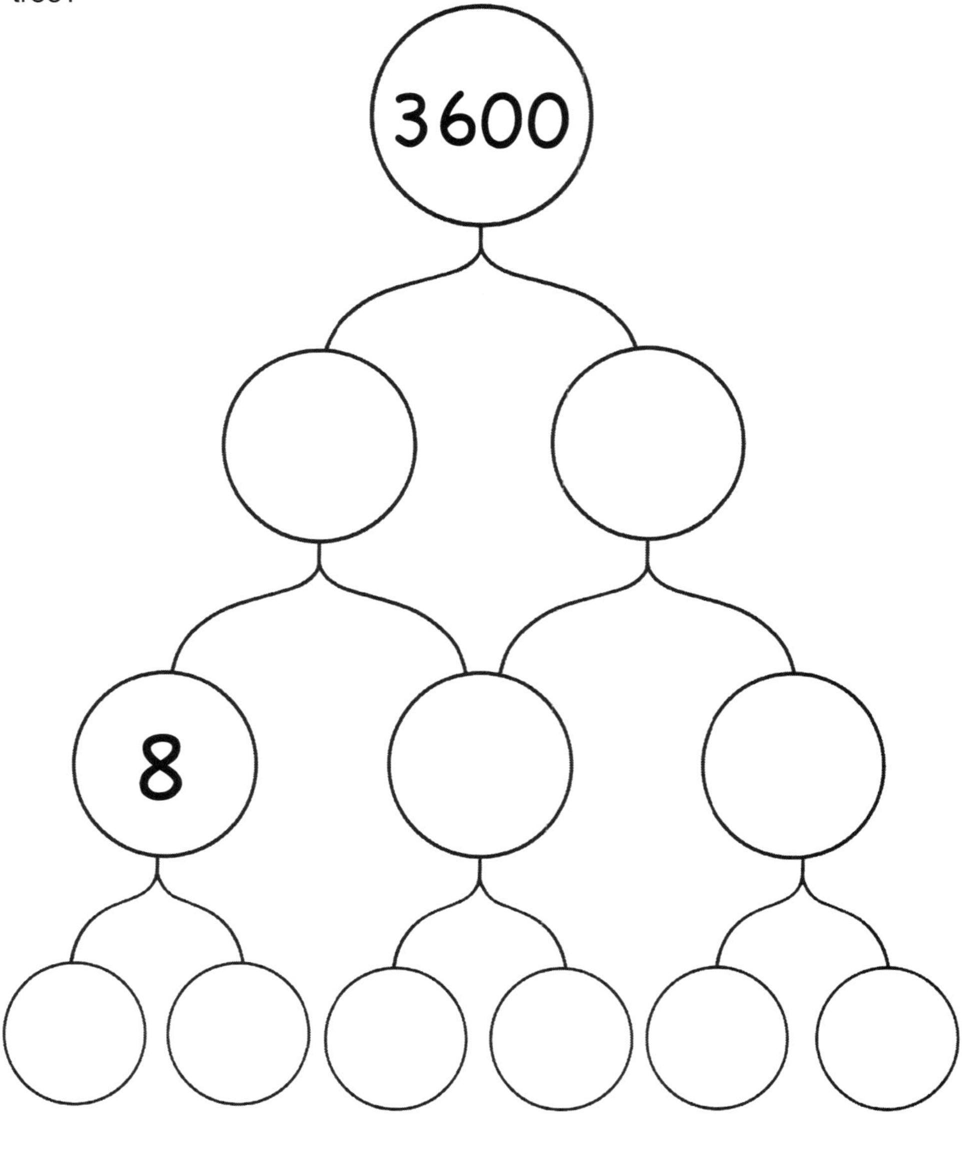

Opposite Crossword

Are you ready for a brain exercise? All the clues for this crossword puzzle are the opposite of the answers.

DOWN		ACROSS	
2	North	1	Pull
3	Open	4	Sink
6	No	5	Beautiful
8	Inside	7	Rough
9	Hot	12	Big
10	Front	13	Start
11	Lose	14	Old
12	Long	15	Thin

9X9 Sudoku

Place numbers in the empty squares so that every row, column, and box with thicker lines includes the numbers 1 to 9.

	4	9		8				7
		8				6		3
		5		7				
7	5	4	1	2				8
	6	1			3	2	7	4
		2				9	1	
			9	6	8	4	3	
4		3				8		
2			5		4			

Spot the difference

Find the 10 differences between these two pictures.

Numberlink

Draw lines to connect each pair of the same numbers. The lines must follow the grid (no diagonal lines), and they must not intersect or touch each other.

A

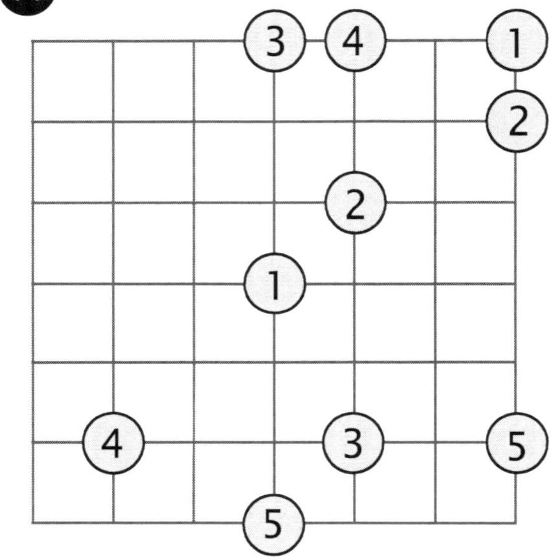

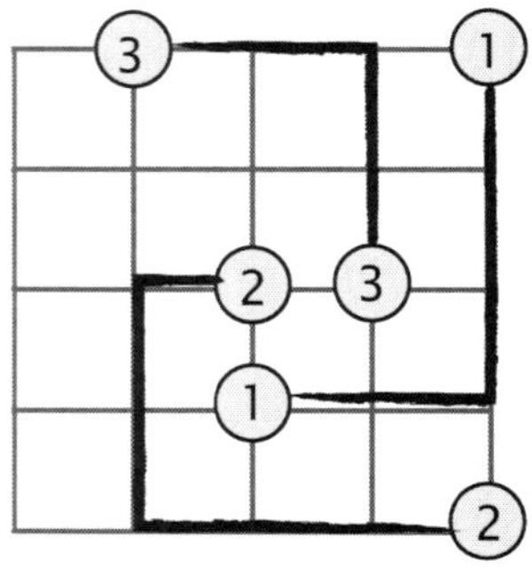

THIS EXAMPLE SHOWS HOW IT WORKS

B

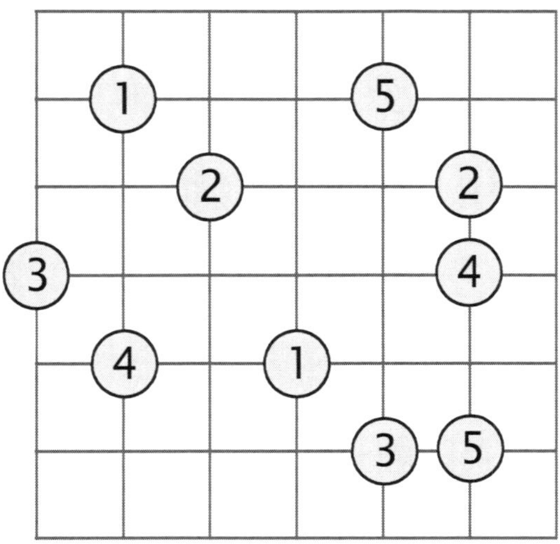

Word Search

Find all these hidden words. They might be written horizontally or vertically, and either forwards or backwards.

CAMERA	MAP
BACKPACK	TRAIN
POSTCARD	HOTEL
TICKET	LANDMARK
SUITCASE	PILOT

P	H	Z	L	A	N	D	M	A	R	K	C	I	F	N
H	T	O	R	C	O	A	N	U	T	H	C	I	X	I
N	L	C	A	M	E	R	A	E	A	K	B	L	U	A
B	E	W	G	U	L	N	Z	M	A	A	X	F	I	R
X	T	E	C	S	T	E	T	O	L	I	P	L	J	T
K	P	M	V	U	X	L	R	Y	B	K	D	I	Q	B
F	H	G	W	I	R	P	O	S	T	C	A	R	D	L
B	W	X	U	T	F	E	Q	B	Q	C	D	G	G	X
A	E	F	C	C	M	C	H	I	Z	J	T	K	B	P
C	G	R	O	A	W	T	O	N	M	L	H	C	T	V
K	D	K	A	S	E	J	I	M	U	D	M	L	E	U
P	P	R	G	E	T	X	R	A	U	V	I	Q	K	U
A	T	P	K	C	P	Z	H	P	S	B	N	L	C	Q
C	X	L	E	T	O	H	O	Q	M	W	I	Q	I	L
K	W	H	Y	L	V	I	O	B	R	O	Z	J	T	S

Puzzle 47

Arranging Dominoes

Can you arrange the dominoes below to fit into the grid? The number of dots on the domino must match the number in the grid, and the dominoes must not overlap with each other. The first one is done for you.

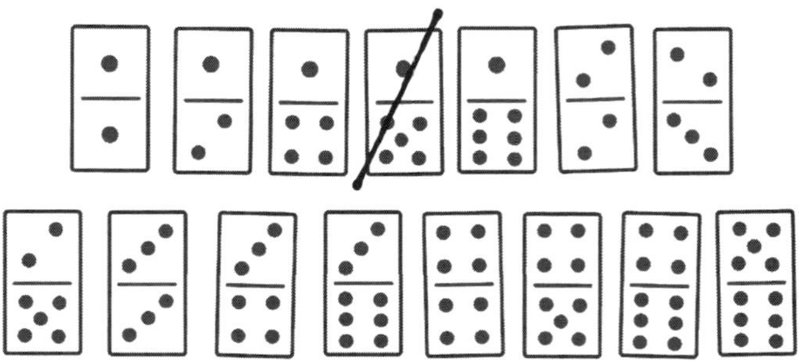

3	5	2	1	1	4
6	2	4	6	1	4
6	1	4	5	2	3
2	1	5	5	3	4
2	3	4	6	3	1

Alphabet Maze

Start from A, can you find the way to Z following the order of the alphabet? You can go vertically, horizontally and diagonally.

W	S	K	G	J	E	D	E	A	B	E
X	M	J	L	F	A	G	C	B	C	F
Z	J	I	K	H	B	D	N	C	K	D
L	K	L	H	G	M	E	M	R	D	O
M	L	N	I	H	F	L	F	K	B	E
T	M	O	T	C	G	O	C	G	F	K
N	R	Q	E	H	D	N	A	H	B	G
M	O	R	F	T	X	M	F	J	K	J
Q	P	S	R	S	T	U	V	W	A	M
R	S	Q	S	K	T	H	M	D	K	O
T	T	W	R	X	M	U	L	T	Q	R
R	U	Y	Y	Q	V	G	V	S	T	W
V	W	T	X	W	X	W	Y	W	X	Y
Y	Z	Y	S	X	Y	D	A	Y	S	T

Puzzle 49

Which Country?

Which country is this airplane going to? Solve the puzzles with the clues below and read the answer in the highlighted column. All clues are a form of transportation.

Clues:

1 Runs on rails

2 Long road vehicle to carry passengers

3 Ride for a snowy day down the hills

4 Vehicle for traveling on water

5 Four-wheeled road vehicle

6 Travel on foot

7 Sky transportation

8 Vehicle with pedals

9 Farmer's vehicle

Missing Numbers

The grids below are missing some numbers. Can you put numbers 1,2,3,4, or 5 in the empty squares so that every row and every column in both grids contain all five numbers.

A

	5	2		4
1				2
		3		
4				3
5		4		1

B

			3	2
5	3			
			5	3
3	4			
			1	4

Crack the Passcode

Can you figure out the three-digit passcode? Check out the attempts below, you'll find a ✓ when a number is correct but in a wrong position, and a ★ when a number is correct and in the correct position. Use these clues to find the correct code.

Attempt	Clues
175	★
813	✓ ✓
247	
527	✓
148	✓

Puzzle 52

Spatial Logic

Following the clues given, can you figure out which space each shape should go into in these two puzzles?

A

1. The triangle is only next to the circle
2. The square is in between the star and the circle
3. There's nothing on the left of the star

B

1. The star is in between the circle and the square
2. The circle is not next to the triangle
3. The square is on the right of the triangle

Finding Pairs

Can you find 5 pairs of identical vehicles in the picture below?

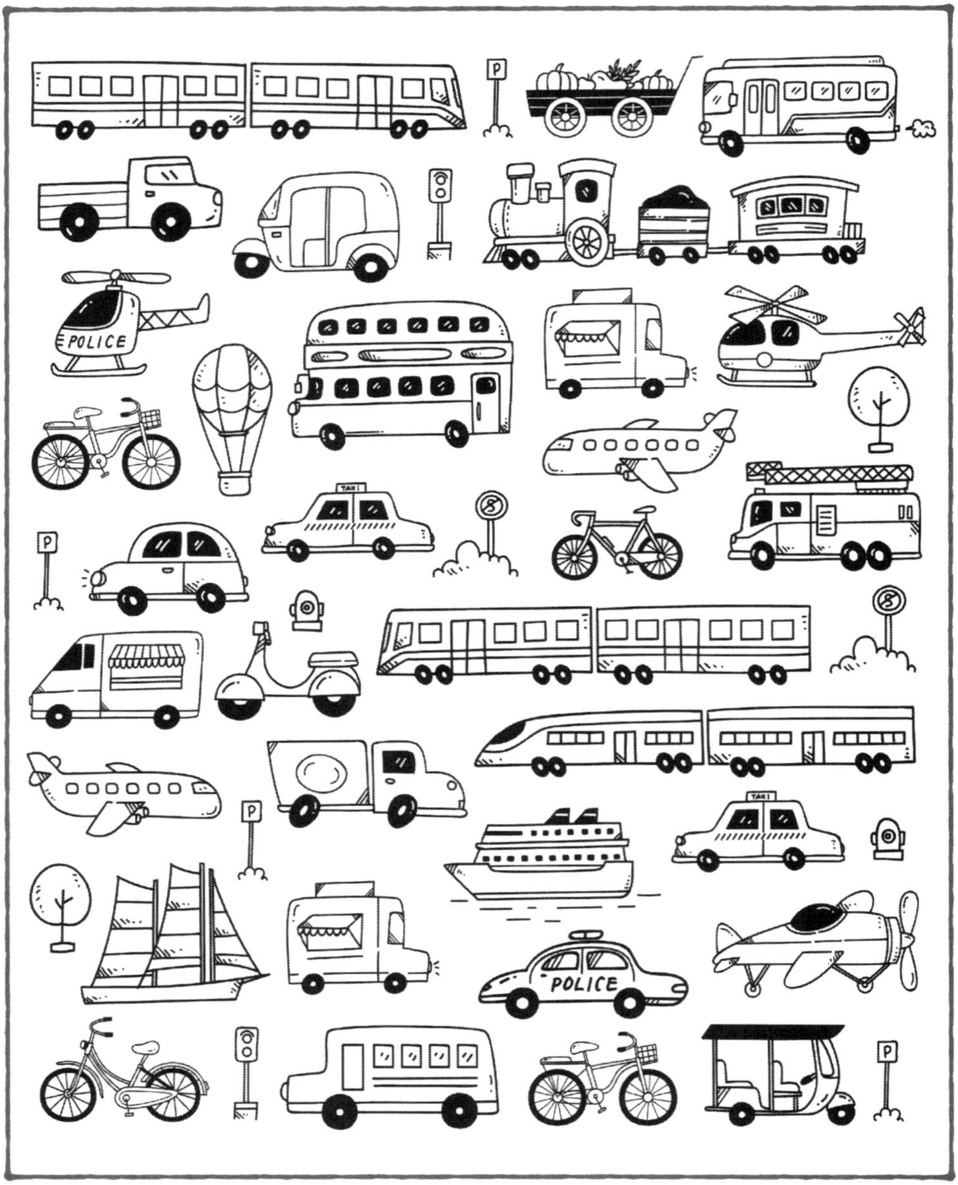

9X9 Sudoku

Place numbers in the empty squares so that every row, column, and box with thicker lines includes the numbers 1 to 9.

			7	4	6	9		8
		4	3		2	5		
8	3	7			9	2		
			6	5	8			
		8	1		7			
1		9			4	6		
	8		4				6	3
	2				1			
	5	6	9	7	3			

Puzzle 55

Airport Logic

Oh no! It's a mess in the airport. Could you use the clues and the grid provided to figure out the answer to these questions?

Where is passenger D traveling to?
What's the colour of passenger C's suitcase?

CLUES:

a. The blue suitcase is going to Mexico
b. A is traveling to France
c. D has a pink suitcase
d. C is not traveling to Mexico
e. B's suitcase is not red nor black
f. The black suitcase is going to Canada
g. A has a red suitcase

		Passenger				Destination			
		A	B	C	D	France	Mexico	Canada	Scotland
Suitcase	Pink						✗		
	Black						✗		
	Red						✗		
	Blue					✗	✓	✗	✗
Destination	France								
	Mexico								
	Canada								
	Scotland								

MAKE A CROSS OR TICK IN THE GRID ACCORDING TO THE CLUES. IT WILL HELP YOU ELIMINATE WRONG ANSWERS. THE FIRST CLUE HAS BEEN MARKED FOR YOU HERE.

Puzzle 56

Word Search

Find these words in the circle below. They might be written horizontally, vertically, or diagonally, and either forwards or backwards.

HAIR	STOMACH	ELBOW	SHOULDER
HEAD	WAIST	KNEE	TOOTH
MOUTH	CHEEK	FOOT	NOSE

H L S J A
U X C V C N E Q N
W Q D A H U K L X B O
R N E T E U I O B O I V S
D H Z J E I T E L O I F Q Y E
H H L H K Z P K T I W H M S H J U
C S V J C V B N M W Y K I M A D Y
G A B Z C K J I W O U N W Y D I Q H G
D M S D N F G H J K E L Z L I R Y T D
E O F T S I A W Y E F B K N D G X O E
C T G G H J K L U B V D S H K G L O C
S Z B H S I T E D H E A D N G D T
Y B N R T R E W C B N M K I Q P U
H X M A W F S H O U L D E R O
Z E O O U Y B J F C V U R
G T U G T I E M C T D
Q A T D E T O O F
R H C Y U

Puzzle 57

Weather Sequence

What weather symbol comes next?

A

B

C

D

E

Puzzle 59

Weather Crossword

Search your brain for weather-related words!

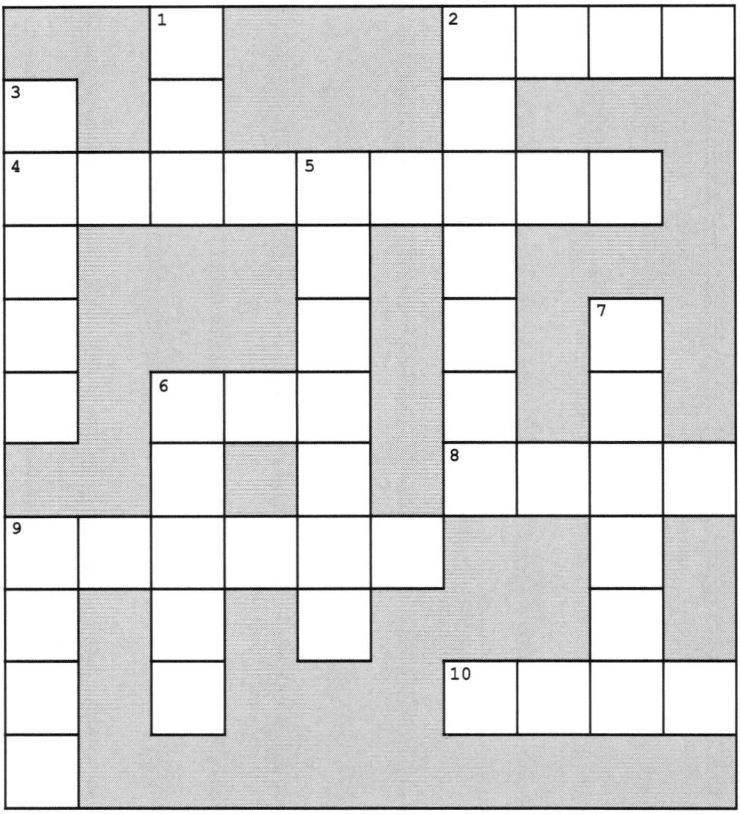

DOWN

1 Thick cloud near the ground

2 Colourful arc in the sky

3 Fluffy thing in the sky

5 The loud noise or low distant rumble from the sky

6 Violent outburst of bad weather

7 The coldest season of the year

9 Falling white flakes

ACROSS

2 Drops of water falling from the sky

4 Bright flash or streak of light in the sky

6 The star of our solar system

8 Movement of air

9 Short burst of rain

10 Comfortable temperature, not too hot

Puzzle 60

Arranging Dominoes

Can you arrange the dominoes below to fit into the grid? The number of dots on the domino must match the number in the grid, and the dominoes must not overlap with each other.

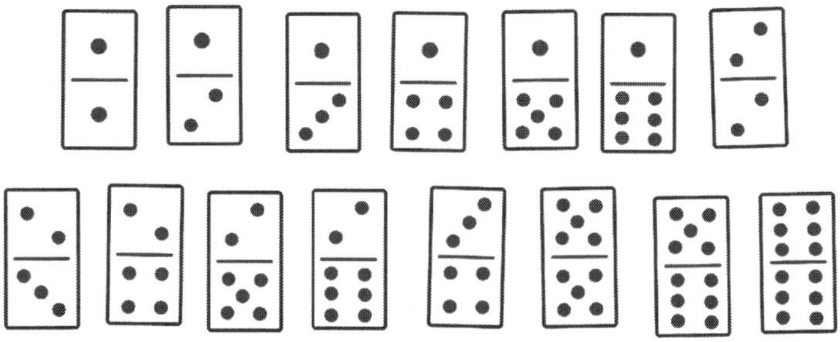

6	4	2	2	2	1
6	3	1	5	5	1
5	4	1	2	6	3
5	6	2	3	1	2
1	6	4	1	5	2

Spot the difference

Can you find the 10 differences between these two pictures?

Puzzle 62

Broken Words

Oops, this winter holiday packing list has been torn apart. Could you figure out what was on the list? You can find clues from pictures on this page.

muffs

so

sca

glo

ater

ves

swe

rf

ear

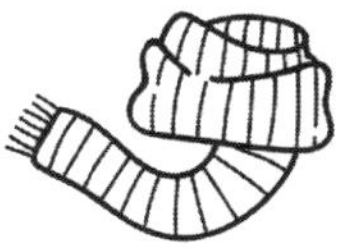

cks

ket

tens

ots

mit

jac

bo

1 ____________________

5 ____________________

2 ____________________

6 ____________________

3 ____________________

7 ____________________

4 ____________________

8 ____________________

Puzzle 63

Word Jigsaw

Is it going to be nice weather for camping? Solve this word jigsaw to find out. Write the letters from the jigsaw pieces below into the correct squares, then read the answer.

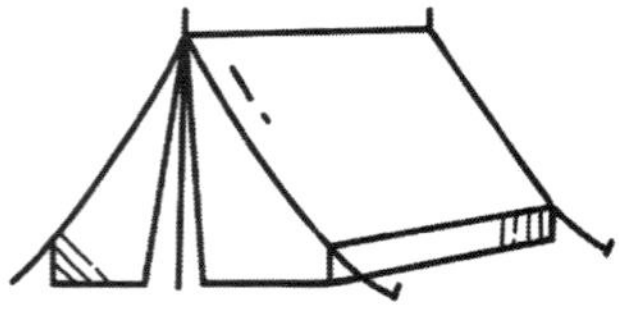

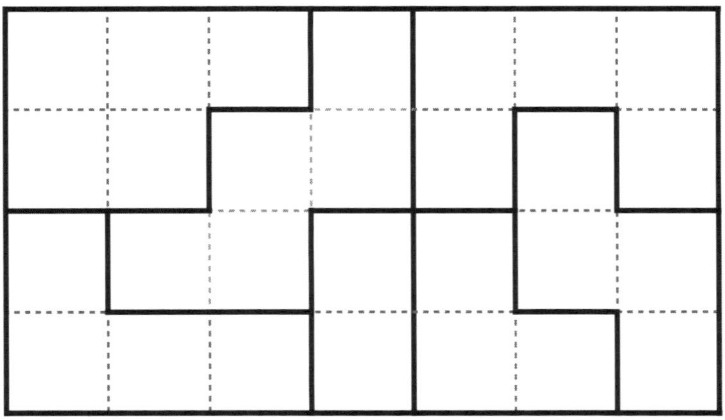

Write it down here

Missing Numbers

The grids below are missing some numbers. Can you put numbers 1,2,3,4, or 5 in the empty squares so that every row and every column in both grids contain all five numbers.

A

2		1	3	
	2		4	3
4		3		1
5	3		1	
	1	2		4

B

	3		5	
5		4		1
	4		1	
2		3		5
	5		2	

Season Puzzle

Four children are talking about their preferred season and they all have a different preference. Can you figure out which season each of them likes the most?

Bridge Puzzle

Draw bridges between islands so the number of bridges connected to each island matches the number on the island.

Rules:

a. The bridges must be straight lines without bends

b. The bridges can not intersect with each other

c. The bridges can be horizontal or vertical but not diagonal

d. The maximum number of bridges between two islands is 2

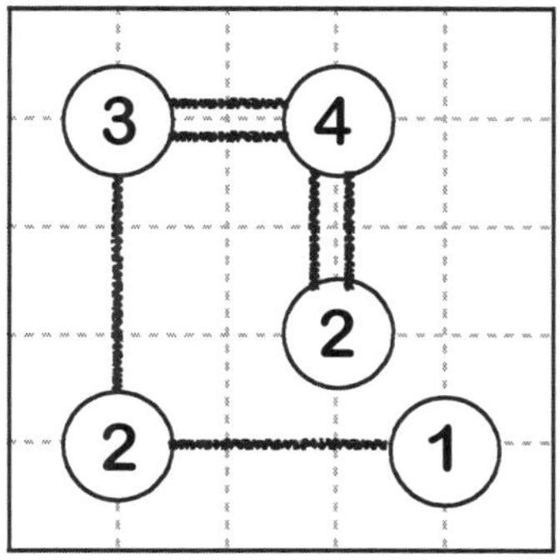

THIS EXAMPLE SHOWS HOW IT WORKS

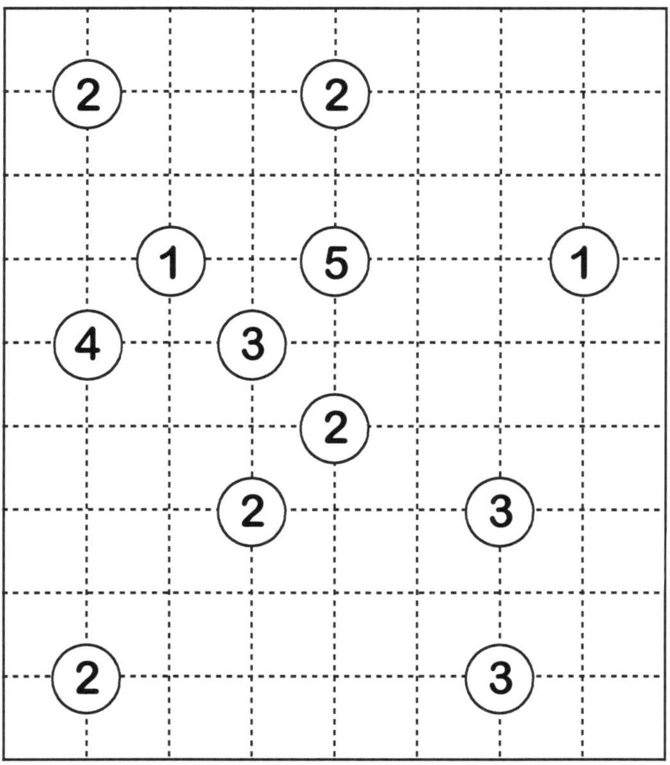

Number Pyramid

In this pyramid, the number in each square is the sum of the two numbers below it. Can you fill in all the empty squares?

163					
	42				
	18				
		11			
			8		6

ICE CREAM TIME!
A
B
C
ICE CREAM

Domino Puzzle

Can you place these domino pieces in the grey spaces below to complete the domino chain? Each domino has two halves, only the halves with the same number can touch each other.

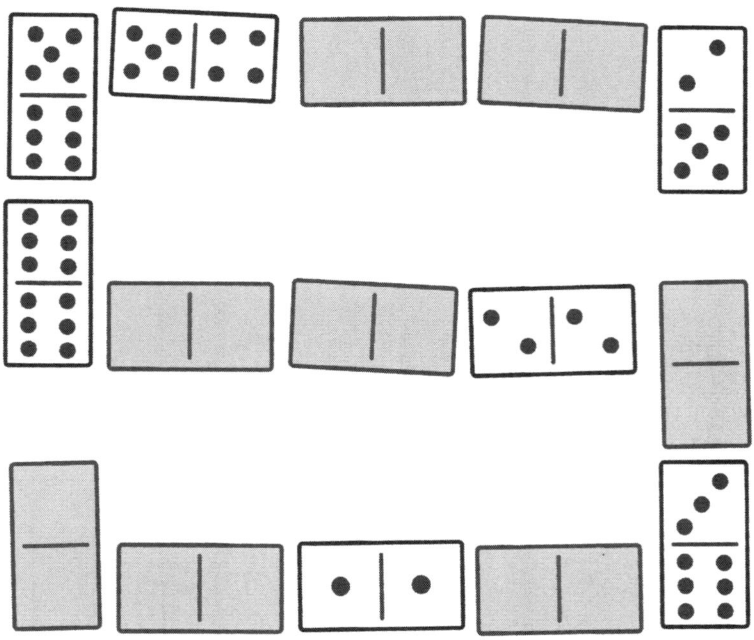

Kyudoku Puzzle

Select numbers 1 to 9 in the grid so that in each row and column the sum of the selected numbers adds up to 9 or less. Each number can only be selected once.

9	1	6	7	7	2
9	5	1	8	2	6
1	5	2	3	3	7
6	2	6	5	6	3
7	9	4	6	7	9
7	6	9	5	3	7

1. In the puzzle above, the correct 1 has been found so all other 1s in the grid can be crossed out as they no longer can be part of the solution.
2. Eliminate those numbers that would make a column or row to add up to more than 9.
3. If there is a number that appears only once in the grid, it must be the correct one.

Spot the Impossible

The shape below makes a six-sided cube. Can you observe the patterns on the cubes and spot the one that is impossible to be made from this shape?

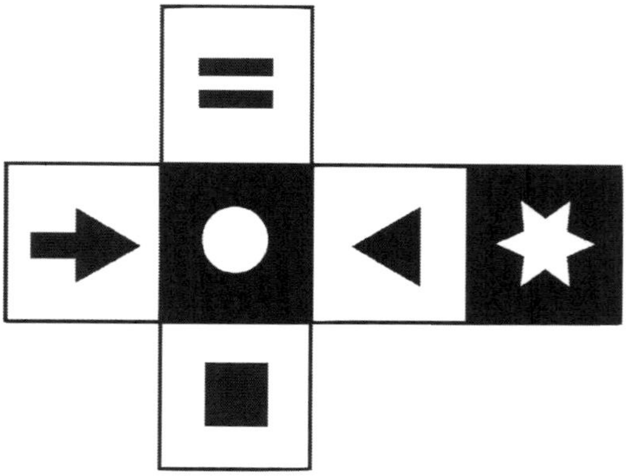

(A)

(B)

(C)

(D)

(E)

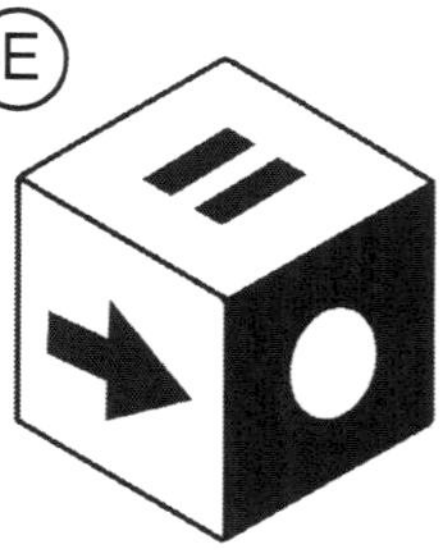

(F)

Crack the Passcode

Can you figure out the three-digit passcode? Check out the attempts below, you'll find a ✓ when a number is correct but in a wrong position, and a ★ when a number is correct and in the correct position. Use these clues to find the correct code.

Attempt	Clues
637	✓ ✓
325	✓
198	
721	★
683	✓

?	?	?

Puzzle 73

Treasure Hunt

Treasure has been hidden in the playground. Work out the missing letters in the word puzzles below and cross out the corresponding row or column on the map. The map square left open is where the treasure is hidden!

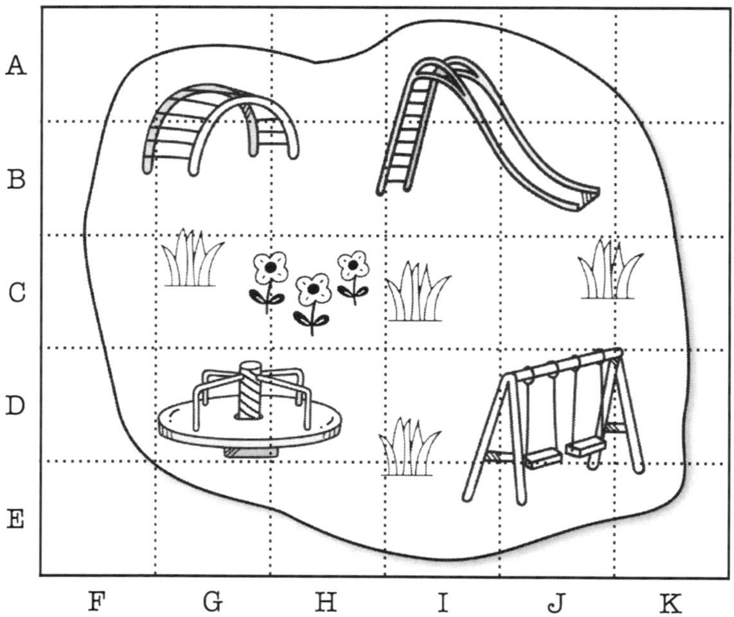

__ENCH

__ITE

__OG

__R__SS

__LOWER

SL__D__

__OGGING

9X9 Sudoku

Place numbers in the empty squares so that every row, column, and box with thicker lines includes the numbers 1 to 9.

6	3			9		7		1
4					1			
7				2		4	8	
	2	7	8	1				
8	6	3	5		2		1	
	5	4	9				3	
5	7			8	4		2	
2	1		3		7	8	6	
					9			

Puzzle 75

Number Maze

Starting from 1, find the way to 30. You can go vertically, horizontally and diagonally.

5	4	2	1	2	3	5	7
6	5	2	2	8	4	2	6
2	4	3	3	7	5	10	11
3	5	1	6	7	9	8	12
6	8	6	7	8	10	10	13
9	7	7	15	12	11	13	14
5	6	21	18	10	17	15	16
20	21	20	19	12	16	15	17
22	23	24	18	17	18	13	18
23	30	22	25	18	19	15	19
24	24	21	27	18	22	17	16
25	20	25	26	29	28	27	25
30	26	28	27	28	29	26	21
29	25	24	30	29	22	23	26

Birthday Crossword

Search your brain for birthday and party related words!

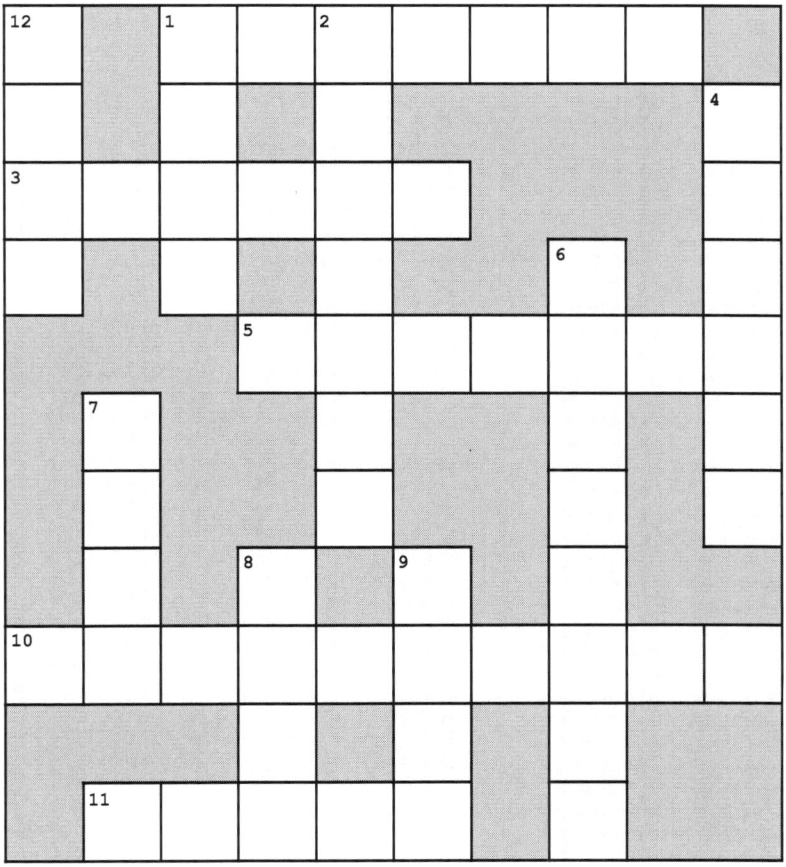

DOWN

1 The word a person is known by

2 Inflatable toy or decoration

4 A person you know well and like and who likes you too

6 An unexpected event

7 Birthday party treat with candles

8 A baby was ____ when the mum gave birth

12 A present

ACROSS

1 Small party food

3 Group of people who are related to each other, such as parents and their children

5 Fancy dress outfit

9 Musical chairs, or pass the parcel

10 Christmas tree trimmings

11 Move rhythmically to music

Spatial Logic

Following the clues given, can you figure out which space each shape should go into?

A

1. The circle is only next to the triangle
2. The star is in between the triangle and the square
3. The square is in between the star and the arrow
4. There's nothing on the left of the arrow

B

1. The circle is only next to the arrow
2. The triangle is in between the star and the square
3. The square is right in the middle
4. There's nothing on the left of the star

Spot the difference

Find the 10 differences between these two pictures.

Puzzle 79

Arrow Words

Could you solve this word puzzle? The clues are in the grey squares, and the arrows from the clue point to the squares where the answer words should go. All the words go from left to right, or top to bottom, no matter which direction the arrow points. Some clues are pictures!

An area with lots of trees					
What chips and french fries are made of		To pull along			
			What we need to do when we're hungry		Use oars to move a boat Excuse ___ !
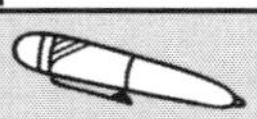 One of many on a zebra		Greetings!		The smallest component of an element	

Futoshiki Puzzle

Fill in numbers in the empty squares so that every row and column includes the numbers 1, 2, 3, and 4. Use the inequality signs as clues and make sure the numbers obey the inequality sign between them. The pointy arrow between two numbers always points at the smaller one.

A

2						
V		V				
		3	>			
		2	>			

CHECK OUT PUZZLE 13 FOR EXAMPLES AND TIPS TO SOLVE FUTOSHIKI PUZZLES.

B

						2
2	>			4		
						V
		2				

Puzzle 81

Multiplication Tree

In the multiplication tree, the numbers in the circles are the multiplication product of the two numbers that are connected below. The bottom row of this tree contains the numbers 1 to 6, each only appears once. Could you work out the remaining numbers in the tree?

A CALCULATOR MIGHT BE HANDY

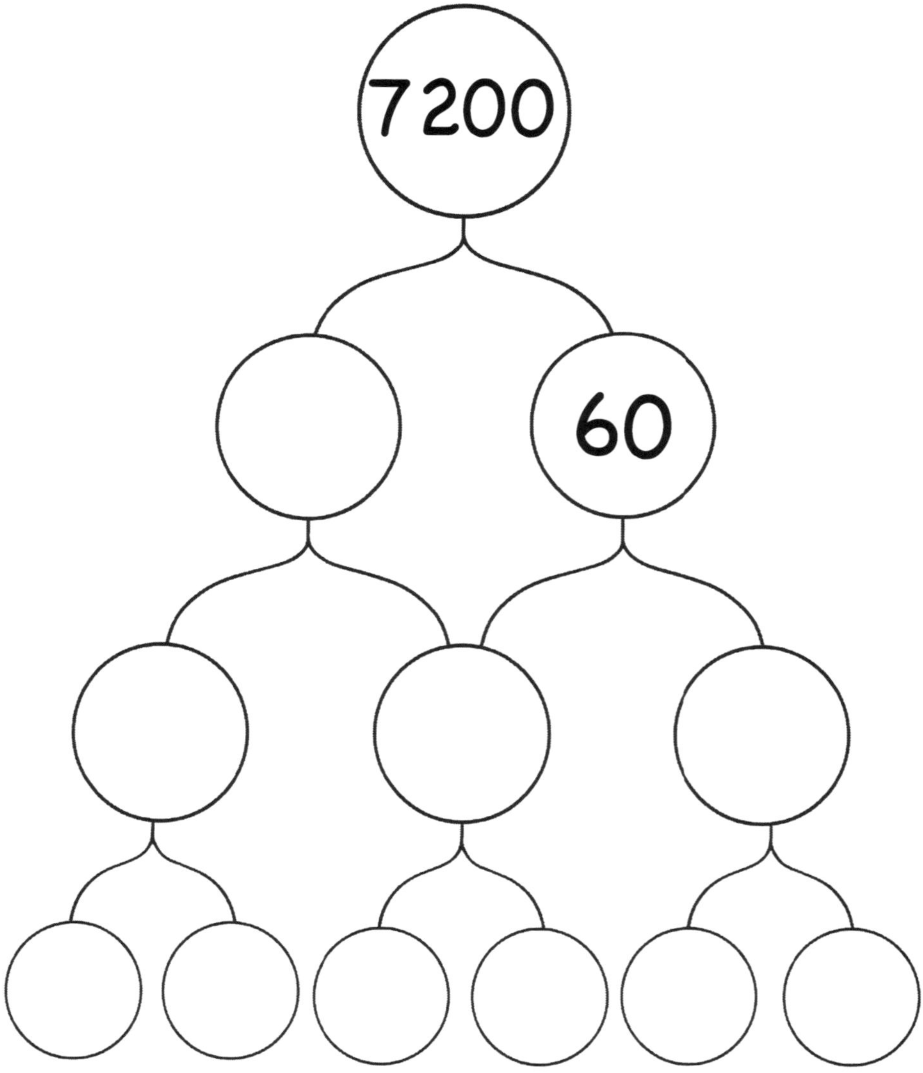

Number Cross

Can you fit all the numbers into their proper places in the grid below? They can go left to right or top to bottom. Two numbers have been revealed to help get you started.

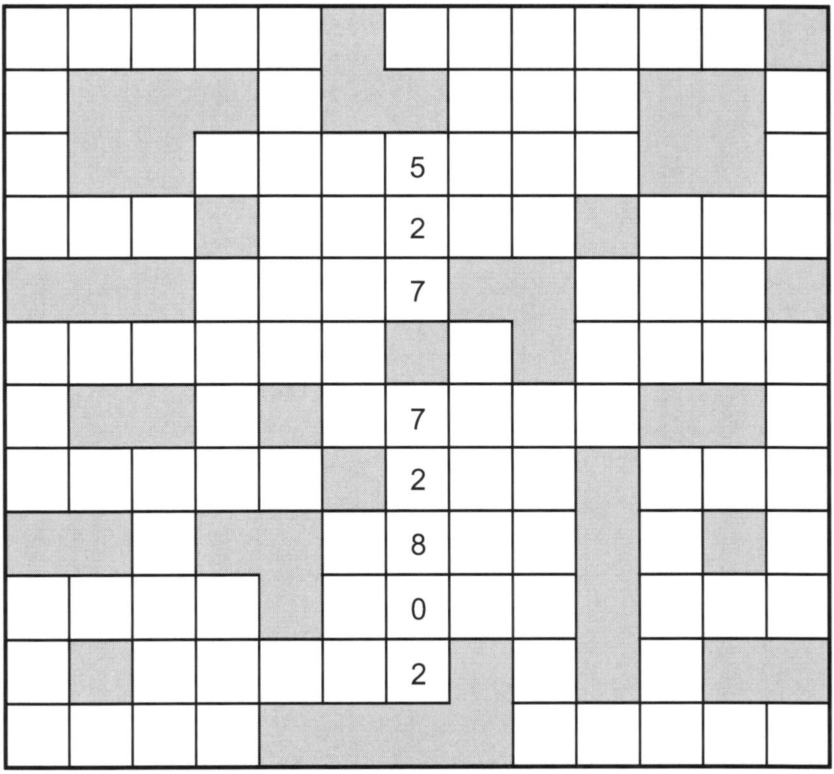

3 Digits

048
097
230
262
329
335
348
371
439
501
515
~~527~~
628
641
917
932
936

4 Digits

0024
0521
0687
1357
1521
3180
4490
5490
5863
8608

5 Digits

10892
20362
23280
37057
43843
52167
68932
69412
71865
~~72802~~
89715
96235

6 Digits

399594
503439
731269
884523

7 Digits

7145095

Puzzle 83

I Spy

Can you find all these different unicorns and count how many of each are?

Arranging Dominoes

Can you arrange the dominoes below to fit into the grid? The number of dots on the domino must match the number in the grid, and the dominoes must not overlap with each other. The first one is done for you.

6	3	6	6	2	1
4	1	4	5	2	1
6	2	4	6	4	2
3	2	3	5	4	1
6	1	5	5	1	4

Puzzle 85

Instrument Word Search

Can you find all these hidden words? They might be written horizontally, vertically, or diagonally, and either forwards or backwards.

PIANO	TRIANGLE	ACCORDION
CLARINET	HARP	TRUMPET
FLUTE	GUITAR	TUBA
VIOLIN	HARMONICA	BANJO
DRUM	CELLO	UKULELE

```
L B H N J N E C K O K B L J G J N I M X
I A P Z I N L R E Y U I O E T U L F H C
G N J N E A K N D W E D C D F V D G D Y
D J D R R R F T G U I T A R U H H I J C
D O I I M C B G Z S V D H C I V C A C U
D H N J K L V U Y H N B G T R F V C R E
D E U D H U I G D G D G D R V B A C U P
T C H Q T N O E U F D D Z U D F C D H E
G H D F Y D L T U K H T H M F V I G D Y
E F S S M S I G D R U A Q P A Z N T Y X
D R U M D S N W E R D L H E B V O X S F
H B J N K W E K M D D F E T F V M F D Y
F R T V G O G N C N C N Q L U J R I T Z
L O F J L F H D F S S F H F E J A L F H
G H D L R N O I D R O C C A F V H G D Y
N C E T G U L K U C C U Y U F F U Y U J
G C G H J K K M O L I P T R I A N G L E
S W Q A Z W S X E D C V F R T G B N H Y
P I A N O I U L B G T F C D E R F H H Y
J K I J U J J H Y G T F V C D E A B U T
```

Numberlink

Draw lines to connect each pair of the same numbers. The lines must follow the grid (no diagonal lines), and they must not intersect or touch each other.

A

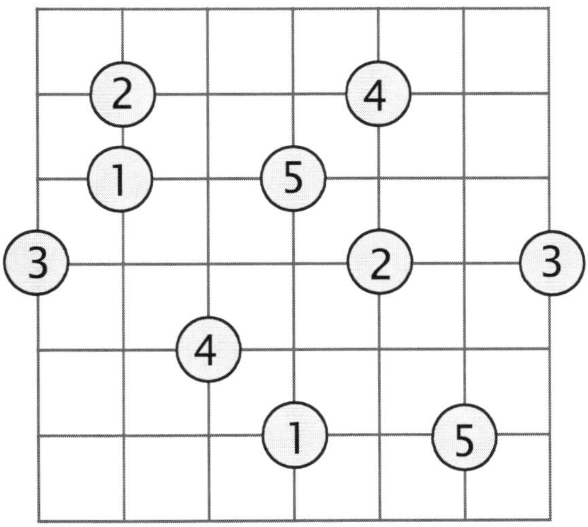

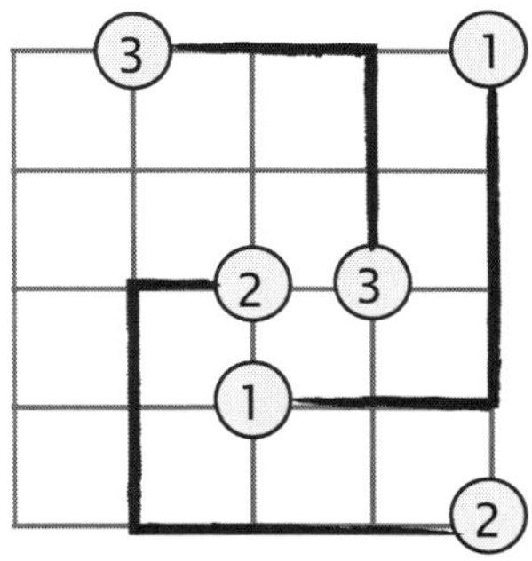

THIS EXAMPLE SHOWS HOW IT WORKS

B

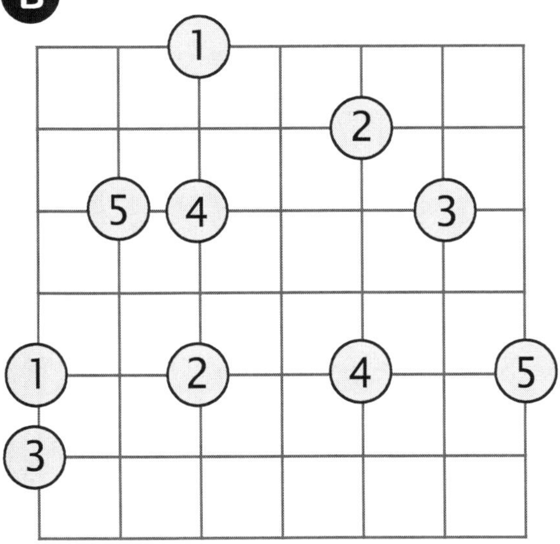

Puzzle 87

Nonogram Password

What's the password to log into this laptop? It's a combination of a word and a 3-digit number. Solve the two nonogram puzzles below and find out.

In a nonogram puzzle, your goal is to find the black squares in the grid and fill them in. The numbers on the top of each column tell you the lengths of continuous black squares in that column, and the numbers on the left of each row are the indications for the lengths of continuous black squares in that row.

Check out *Puzzle 39* for more tips.

	1	5	1	0	5	1 1 1	1 1 1	0	5	1 1	5
3 3 3											
1 1 1 1											
1 3 3											
1 1 1 1											
1 3 1 1											

	1 1 1	1 1 1	5	0	3 1	1 1 1	1 3	0	3 1	1 1 1	5
3 3 3											
1 1 1 1											
3 3 3											
1 1 1											
3 3 3											

Tracing Lines

One of the shapes below is impossible to trace without going over a line twice or taking off your pen. Can you identify it?

A

B

C

D

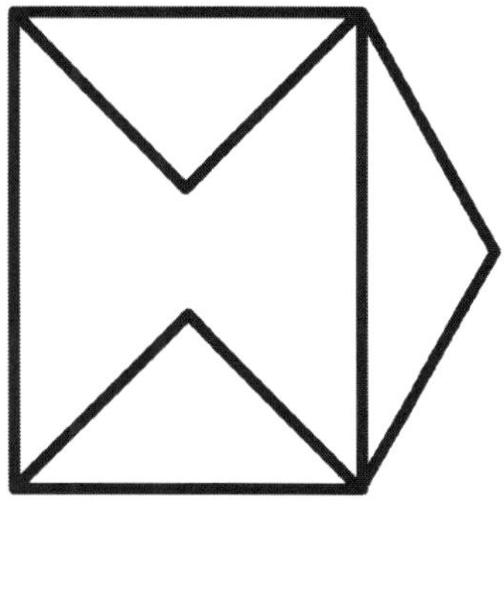

Puzzle 89

PLEASE HELP THE ARMADILLO FIND ITS BURROW!

Arrow Words

Could you solve this word puzzle? The clues are in the grey squares, and the arrows from the clue point to the squares where the answer words should go. All the words go from left to right, or top to bottom, no matter which direction the arrow points. Some clues are pictures!

		Noah's boat			
Period of a year, such as summer or winter		Frozen water			
	____ a cake				
			The largest continent 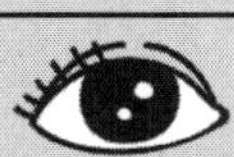		The joint between the thigh and lower leg
	The opposite of NO		A piece of furniture for sleep or rest		

Spot the difference

Find the 10 differences between these two pictures.

Puzzle 92

Broken Shopping List

Oh no, a naughty dog has shredded this shopping list! Could you figure out what was on the list? You can find clues from pictures on this page.

tom

water

car

ad

ato

zza

jui

le

ana

cake

bre

cup

sau

melon

rot

sage

ce

pi

ban

app

1 ____________________

2 ____________________

3 ____________________

4 ____________________

5 ____________________

6 ____________________

7 ____________________

8 ____________________

9 ____________________

10 ____________________

Puzzle 93

Who Does What?

Four kids were talking about their age and their favourite sport. Read what they said and figure out each of their age and favourite sport.

Ben: I am the youngest and my favourite sport is in the water.

Adam: Ben and I don't like basketball and I'm one year older than him.

Daisy: I am one year older than Adam and I know Charlie loves tennis.

Charlie: I am 12 and Ben is 3 years younger than me. I don't like swimming or cycling.

		Child			
Age					
Sport					

THIS CHART MIGHT HELP SORT OUT THE CLUES.

Puzzle 94

Number Triangle

In these triangles, the numbers in the square boxes are the sum of the two numbers in connected circles. For example:

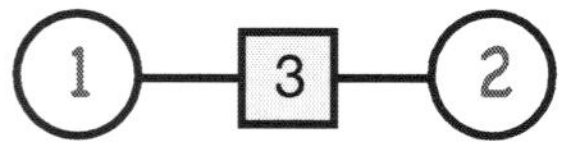

Can you figure out which number should be in each of the circles? They are between 1 to 9 and can only be used once in each triangle.

A

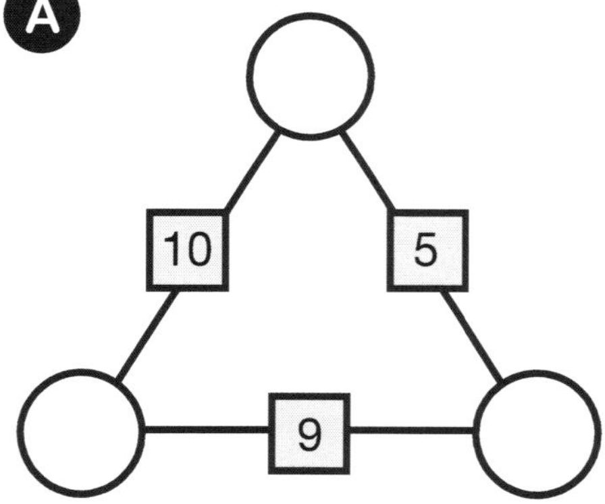

B

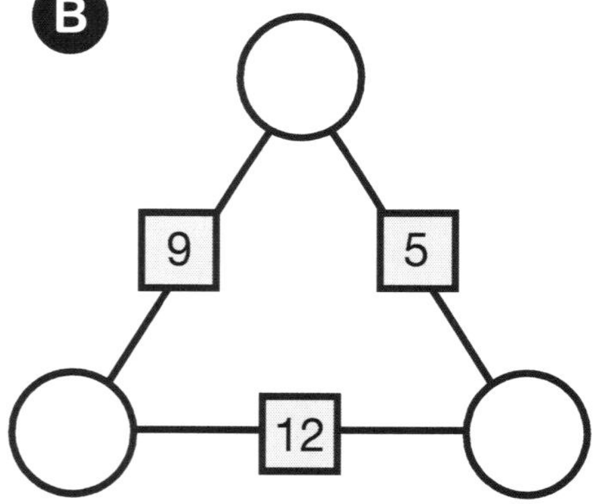

C

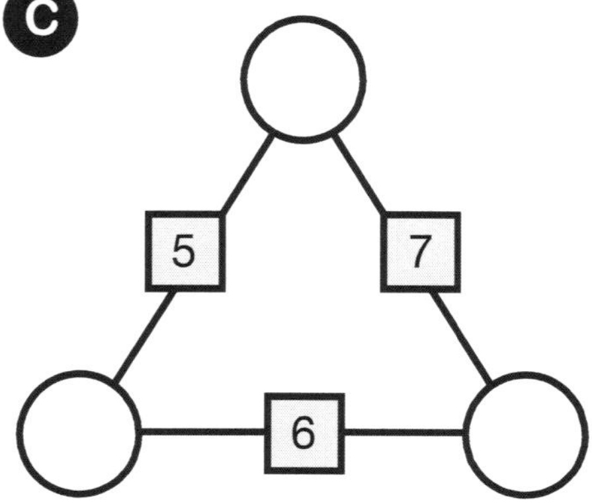

D

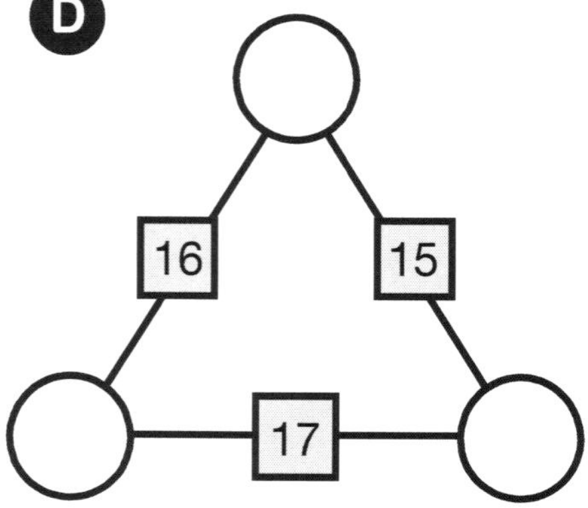

9X9 Sudoku

Place numbers in the empty squares so that every row, column, and box with thicker lines includes the numbers 1 to 9.

					2	3	4	1
7	4			5		2		
		1			4			
5	3			1	6		8	7
		8		4				
						1		4
	8		5	2	9	6		
	1	9				7		8
3	5	6			8		9	

Crack the Code

You are a secret agent and have been given a device. You must log in with a 4-digit passcode to get the information you need.

To crack the code, look up the numbers in the cipher below, choose one of the two letters, and form a word.

For example: 10, 8, 13 = S~~T~~, ~~O~~P, Y~~Z~~ = SPY.

CIPHER

1 = AB	8 = OP
2 = CD	9 = QR
3 = EF	10 = ST
4 = GH	11 = UV
5 = IJ	12 = WX
6 = KL	13 = YZ
7 = MN	

- FIRST DIGIT: 10, 5, 12
- SECOND DIGIT: 10, 3, 11, 3, 7
- THIRD DIGIT: 13, 3, 9, 8
- FOURTH DIGITAL: 3, 8, 11, 9

Which mythical creature?

This mythical creature appears in the folklore of many cultures around the world. Some people believe it brings bad luck, however, there is also a beautiful fairy tale about this creature. Solve the word puzzles below and find out what it is. You'll find the answer in the gray column.

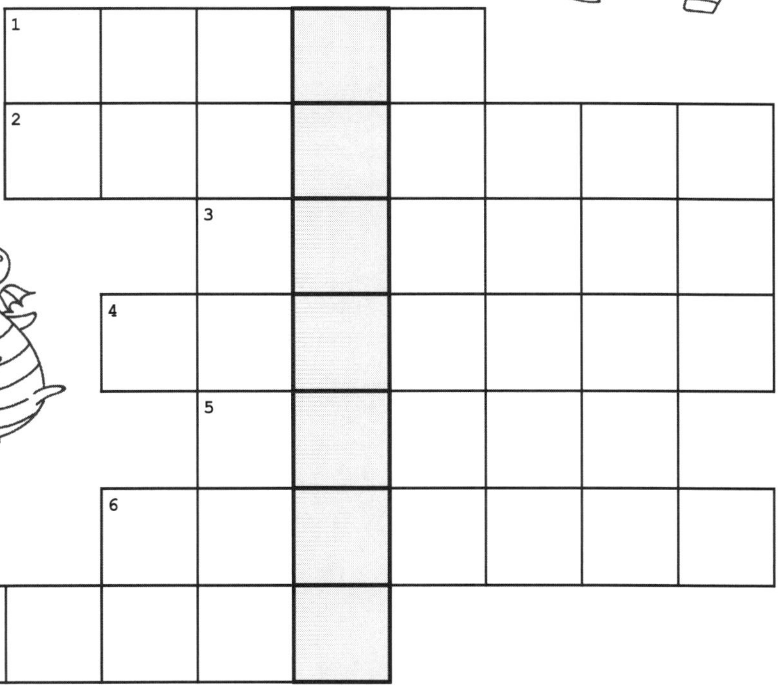

Clues:

1 Small human-like mythical creature in garden

2 Hairy monster that appears at full moon

3 Fire-breathing legendary creature that can fly

4 Blood-sucking monster

5 Tooth collector

6 Scotland's national animal

7 Harry Potter is one

Puzzle 98

Number Cross

Can you fit all the numbers into their proper places in the grid below? Some numbers have been revealed to help get you started.

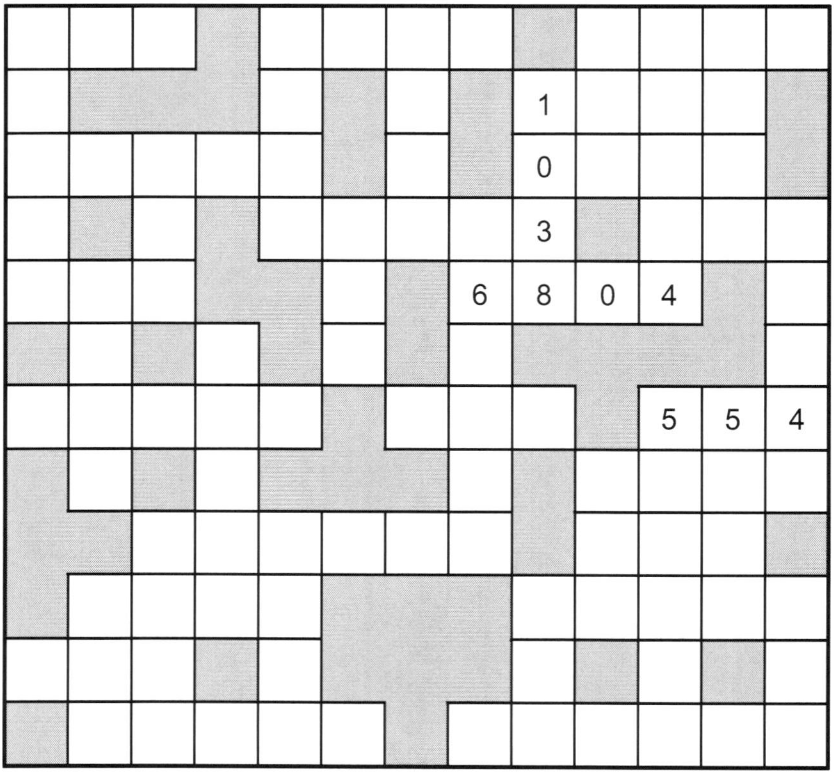

3 Digits

129
226
233
296
301
334
396
523
~~554~~
558
580
637
837
876

4 Digits

0658
~~1038~~
1258
1379
1743
1865
2577
3346
3388
3835
5768
6410
~~6804~~
6872
8731

5 Digits

00649
04145
04567
25843
39683
65379
74554
84983
89042

6 Digits

182960
467390
532663
844381

12 Animals

In the Chinese zodiac, every year is associated with an animal. It cycles every 12 years, starting with the year of the Rat and ending with the year of the Pig.

Reading the clues given by this family and checking out the year chart, can you figure out which year and animal each of them was born in?

Rat	2020	2008	1996	1984	1972
Ox	2021	2009	1997	1985	1973
Tiger	2022	2010	1998	1986	1974
Rabbit	2023	2011	1999	1987	1975
Dragon	2024	2012	2000	1988	1976
Snake	2025	2013	2001	1989	1977
Horse	2026	2014	2002	1990	1978
Goat	2027	2015	2003	1991	1979
Monkey	2028	2016	2004	1992	1980
Rooster	2029	2017	2005	1993	1981
Dog	2030	2018	2006	1994	1982
Pig	2031	2019	2007	1995	1983

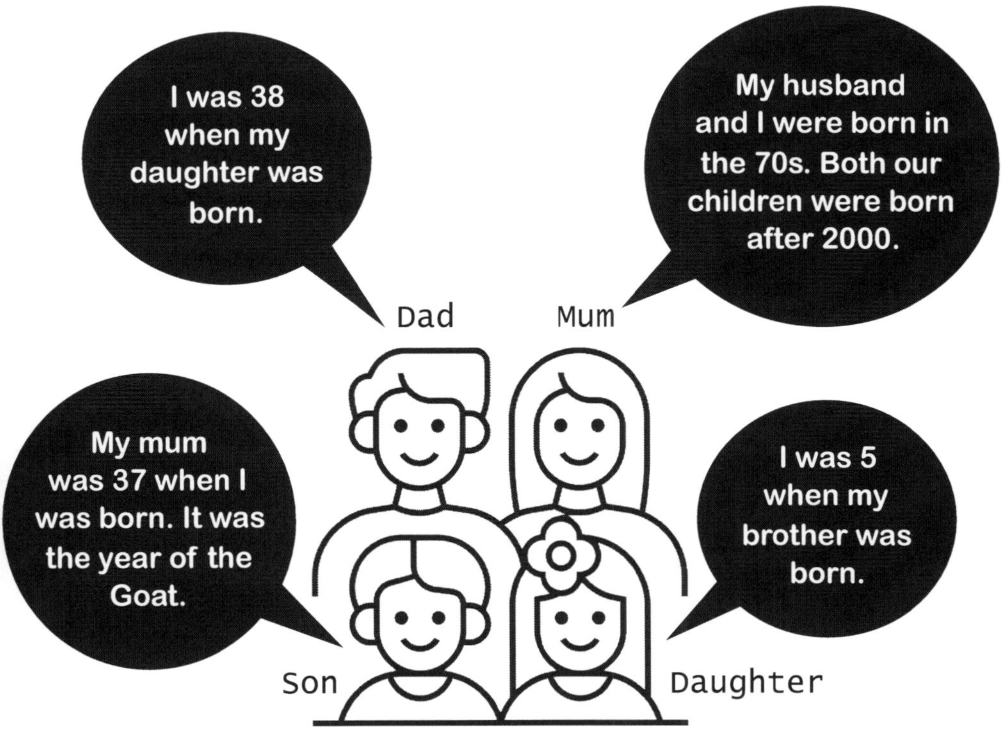

Puzzle 100

Kyudoku Puzzle

Select numbers 1 to 9 in the grid so that in each row and column the sum of the selected numbers adds up to 9 or less. Each number can only be selected once.

4	4	9	7	6	9
6	5	3	6	4	5
5	1	6	8	3	7
9	(7)	5	6	8	2
6	9	4	8	6	9
4	3	1	7	5	6

Tips:

1. In the puzzle above, the correct 7 has been found so all other 7s in the grid can be crossed out as they no longer can be part of the solution.
2. Eliminate those numbers that would make a column or row to add up to more than 9.
3. If there is a number that appears only once in the grid, it must be the correct one.

Spot the difference

Find the 10 differences between these two pictures.

Finding Pairs

Find 5 pairs of identical plants in the picture below.

Bridge Puzzle

Draw bridges between islands so the number of bridges connected to each island matches the number on the island.

Rules:

a. The bridges must be straight lines without bends

b. The bridges can not intersect with each other

c. The bridges can be horizontal or vertical but not diagonal

d. The maximum number of bridges between two islands is 2

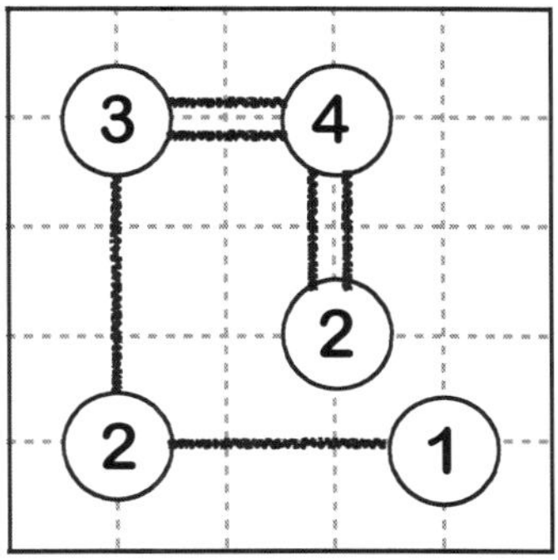

THIS EXAMPLE SHOWS HOW IT WORKS

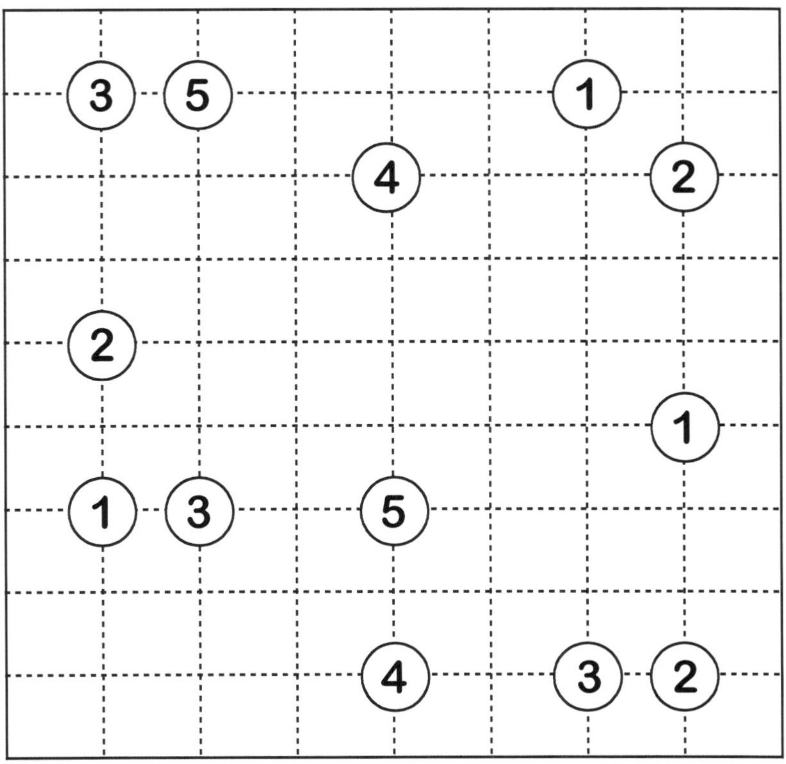

ANSWERS

Answers 1-3

PUZZLE 1

The treasure is hidden in the map square of E and J.

PUZZLE 2

P	N	H	G	E	H	C	A	E	B
I	S	A	O	Z	H	O	V	P	I
H	A	I	L	H	E	F	V	D	O
S	I	D	D	S	V	A	C	M	I
P	L	Z	C	U	A	C	A	A	P
P	O	A	D	T	C	I	P	P	A
H	R	S	D	K	F	S	T	P	R
L	E	G	E	N	D	P	A	M	R
Z	P	M	K	B	H	L	I	S	O
Y	L	A	N	D	E	E	N	N	T

PUZZLE 3

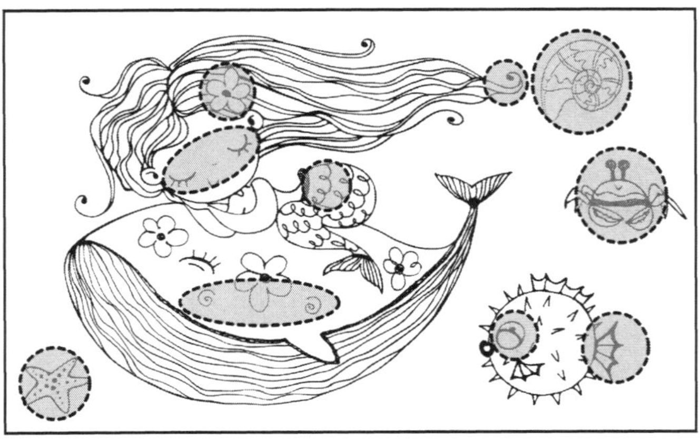

PUZZLE 4

A

3	1	2	4
2	4	1	3
1	3	4	2
4	2	3	1

B

4	3	2	1
2	1	4	3
1	4	3	2
3	2	1	4

C

4	1	3	2
2	3	1	4
1	4	2	3
3	2	4	1

D

3	1	2	4
2	4	1	3
1	3	4	2
4	2	3	1

PUZZLE 5

PUZZLE 6

A 

B 

C 

D 

Answers 7-9

PUZZLE 7 The desert island is the island on the top left of the map.

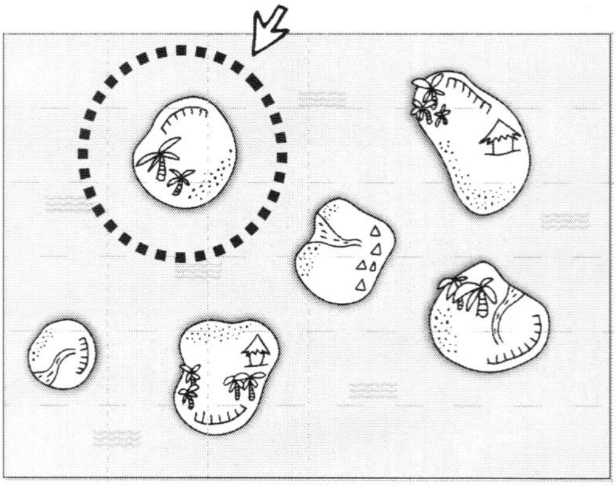

PUZZLE 8 Rope **C** pulls up the anchor.

PUZZLE 9

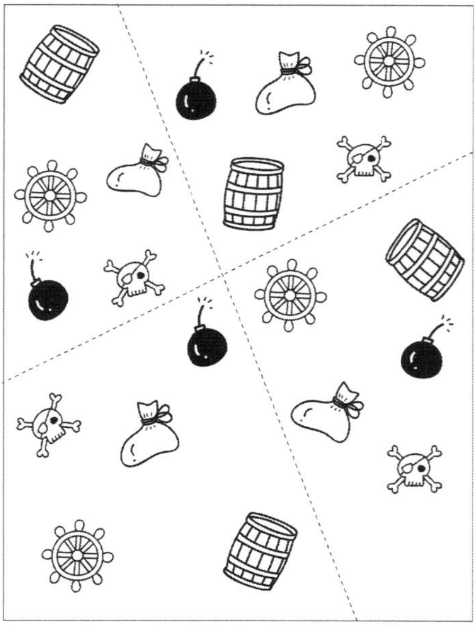

PUZZLE 10

A

1	2	3	4	5
4	1	5	3	2
3	5	4	2	1
5	4	2	1	3
2	3	1	5	4

B

5	3	2	1	4
1	4	5	3	2
2	1	3	4	5
4	5	1	2	3
3	2	4	5	1

PUZZLE 11

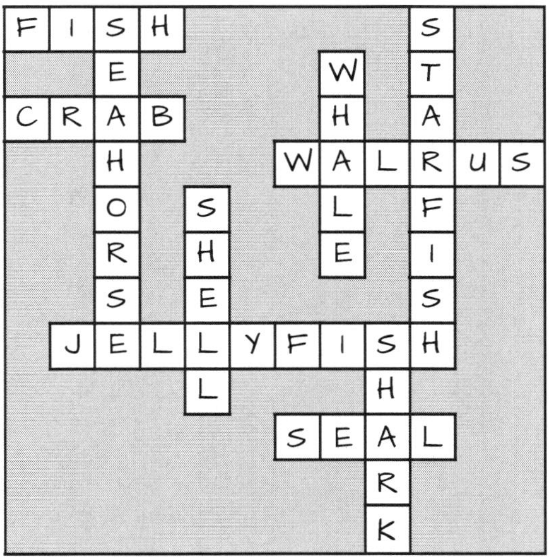

PUZZLE 12

Shape **C** can not be traced without taking the pen off or going over a line twice.

C

Answers 13-16

PUZZLE 13

3	<	4		1		2
		v				
2		3		4		1
1		2	<	3		4
		v		v		
4		1		2	<	3

PUZZLE 14 Chest **B** and **C** hold the real treasure.

PUZZLE 15 Here are the 10 things on the list:

1. ruler
2. scissors
3. crayon
4. globe
5. notebook
6. clock
7. sharpener
8. computer
9. glue
10. pencil

PUZZLE 16

A

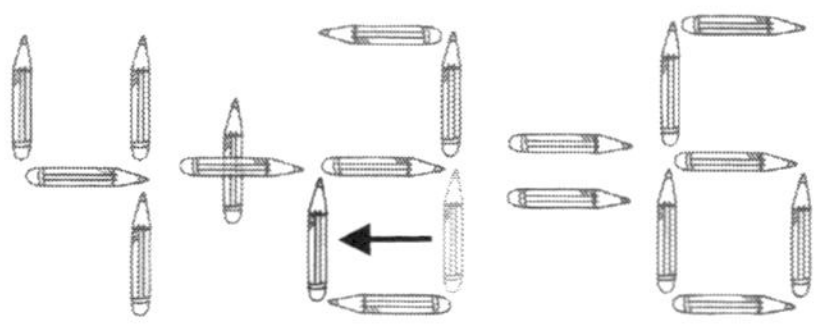

B

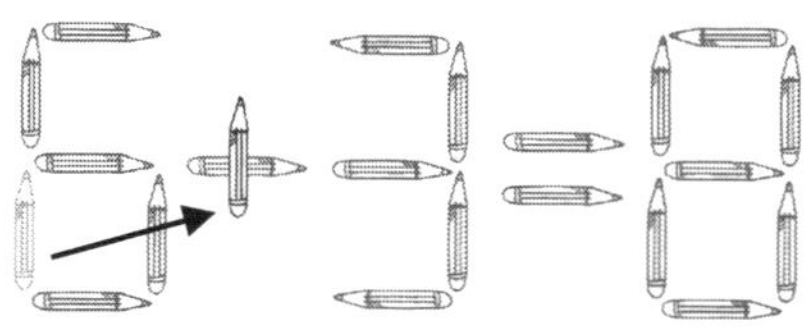

Answers 17-19

PUZZLE 17

The more that you learn the more places you will go.

T	H	E	M	O	R	E
E	R	O	M	T	N	T
P	O	U	E	H	R	H
L	Y	W	L	E	A	A
A	S	I	U	O	Y	T
C	E	L	L	G	O	●

PUZZLE 18

PUZZLE 19

Answers 20-22

PUZZLE 20

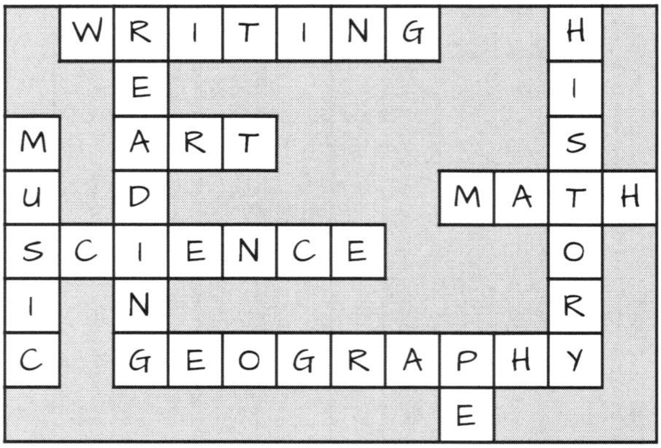

PUZZLE 21

PUZZLE 22

The trophy is in the art room.
The medals are in the garden shed.
The stop watch is in the gym.
The whistles are in the music room.

PUZZLE 23

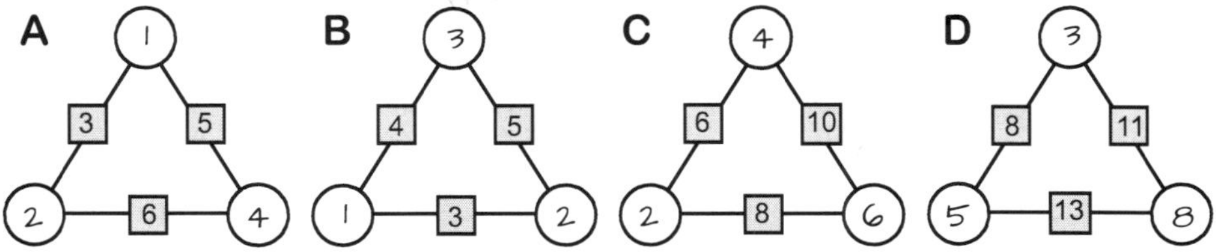

PUZZLE 24

T	W	E	G	E	A	T	L	A	S
A	S	P	A	P	E	R	V	O	I
P	Q	R	L	H	E	F	V	P	J
E	G	R	D	T	V	R	C	O	H
D	L	T	C	Y	Y	E	A	S	M
K	O	O	B	T	N	D	U	T	W
H	R	R	D	D	F	L	T	E	K
L	E	S	A	E	D	O	A	R	S
A	F	S	S	A	S	F	H	H	E
M	A	R	K	E	R	G	N	N	D

PUZZLE 25

A

5	2	1	6	3	4
6	3	4	5	2	1
1	4	6	3	5	2
3	5	2	1	4	6
2	6	3	4	1	5
4	1	5	2	6	3

B

3	1	4	2	6	5
2	6	5	3	1	4
6	4	2	5	3	1
5	3	1	6	4	2
4	2	3	1	5	6
1	5	6	4	2	3

Answers 26-29

PUZZLE 26

David is the oldest and Ben is the youngest.

PUZZLE 27

2	4	1	**6**	**3**	9
3	6	6	9	1	**9**
2	8	**7**	**2**	8	7
8	7	6	4	2	9
1	**4**	6	8	**5**	5
7	8	**1**	8	7	5

PUZZLE 28

		M	O	N	K	E	Y	
		G	O	A	T			
	Z	E	B	R	A			
			O	W	L			
E	L	E	P	H	A	N	T	
			P	A	N	D	A	
		D	O	L	P	H	I	N

PUZZLE 29

PUZZLE 30 The four animal characters are: Dormouse, Cheshire cat, Caterpillar, and White rabbit.

PUZZLE 31 Dad was born in 1982, the year of the Dog.
Mum was born in 1986, the year of the Tiger.
Son was born in 2013, the year of the Snake.
Daughter was born in 2016, the year of the Monkey.

PUZZLE 32

137
68 | 69
37 | 31 | 38
21 | 16 | 15 | 23
10 | 11 | 5 | 10 | 13
1 | 9 | 2 | 3 | 7 | 6

PUZZLE 33

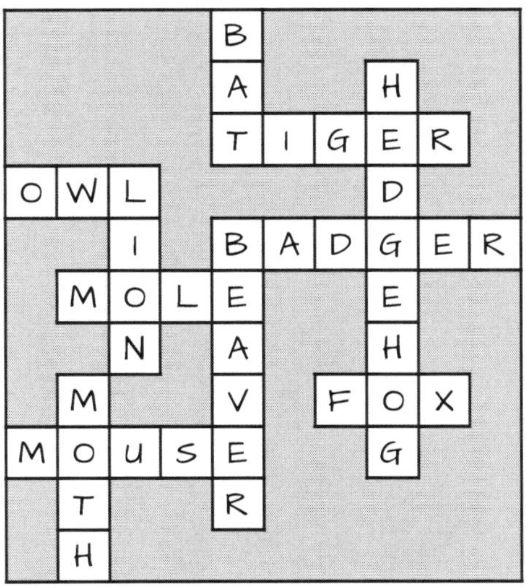

Answers 34-37

PUZZLE 34

PUZZLE 35

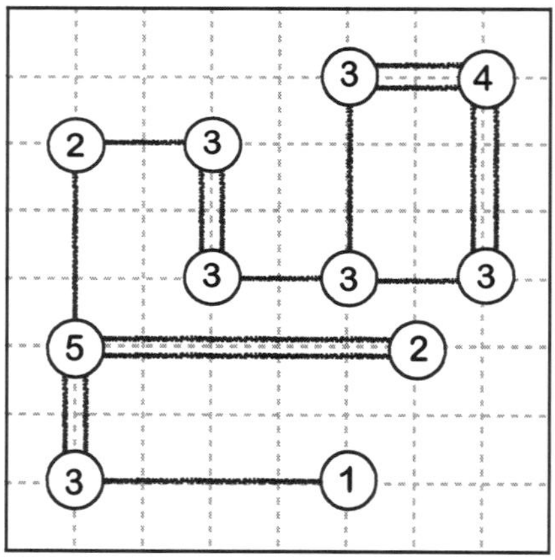

PUZZLE 37

PUZZLE 38

Afternoon	B	A	T	H	
P	E	School gym class	O	How old you are	Fail to win
M	A	M	M	A	L
Animal that produces milk for its young	U	A long time ___	A	G	O
S	T	A	T	E	S
The "S" in U.S.A.	Y	___ and the Beast	O		E

PUZZLE 39

A

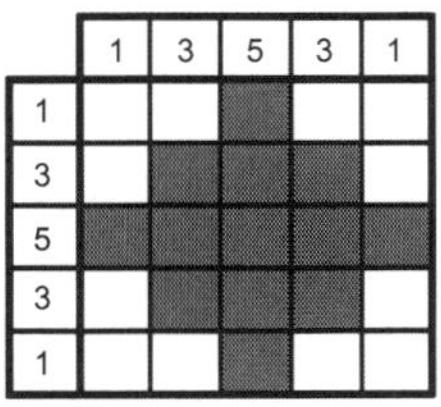

B

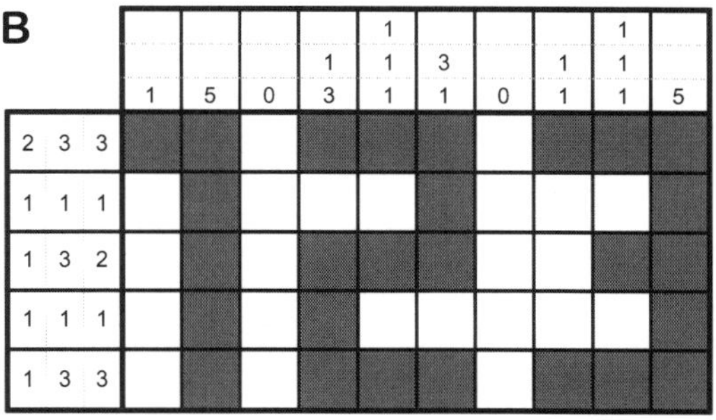

PUZZLE 40

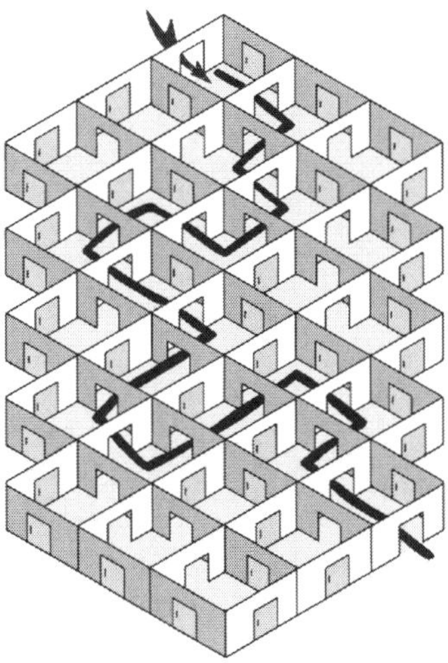

Answers 41-43

PUZZLE 41

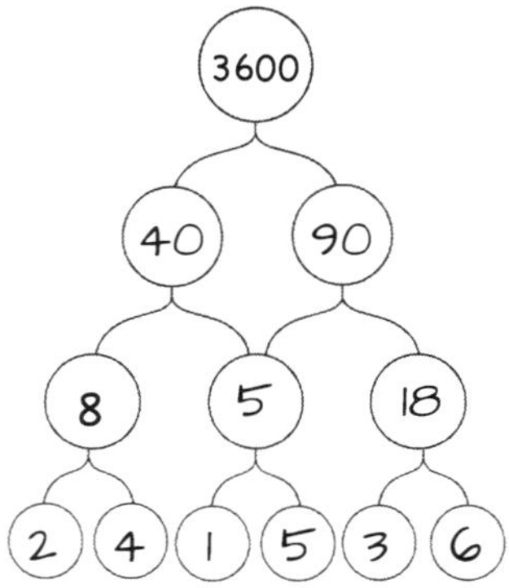

PUZZLE 42

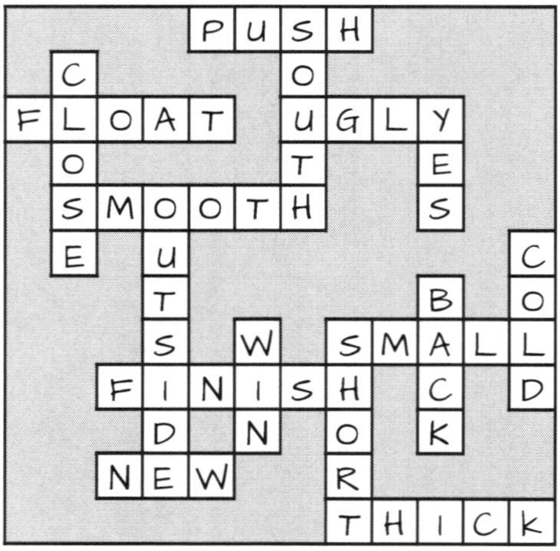

PUZZLE 43

6	4	9	3	8	1	5	2	7
1	7	8	2	9	5	6	4	3
3	2	5	4	7	6	1	8	9
7	5	4	1	2	9	3	6	8
9	6	1	8	5	3	2	7	4
8	3	2	6	4	7	9	1	5
5	1	7	9	6	8	4	3	2
4	9	3	7	1	2	8	5	6
2	8	6	5	3	4	7	9	1

PUZZLE 44

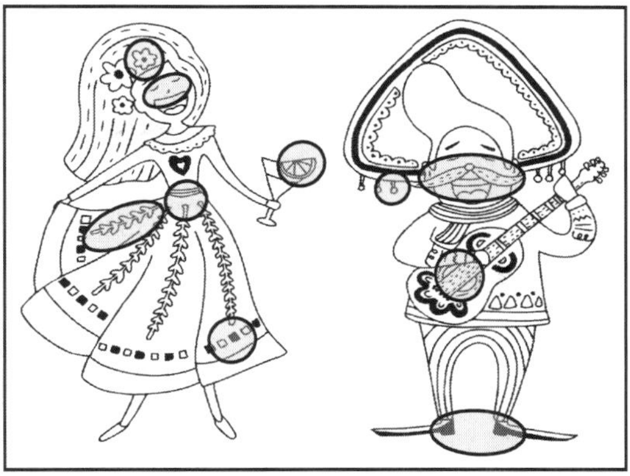

PUZZLE 45

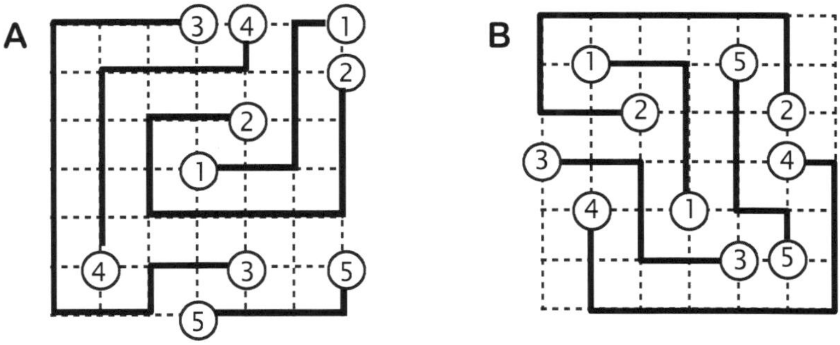

PUZZLE 46

P	H	Z	L	A	N	D	M	A	R	K	C	I	F	N
H	T	O	R	C	O	A	N	U	T	H	C	I	X	I
N	L	C	A	M	E	R	A	E	A	K	B	L	U	A
B	E	W	G	U	L	N	Z	M	A	A	X	F	I	R
X	T	E	C	S	T	E	T	O	L	I	P	L	J	T
K	P	M	V	U	X	L	R	Y	B	K	D	I	Q	B
F	H	G	W	I	R	P	O	S	T	C	A	R	D	L
B	W	X	U	T	F	E	Q	B	Q	C	D	G	G	X
A	E	F	C	C	M	C	H	I	Z	J	T	K	B	P
C	G	R	O	A	W	T	O	N	M	L	H	C	T	V
K	D	K	A	S	E	J	I	M	U	D	M	L	E	U
P	P	R	G	E	T	X	R	A	U	V	I	Q	K	U
A	T	P	K	C	P	Z	H	P	S	B	N	L	C	Q
C	X	L	E	T	O	H	O	Q	M	W	I	Q	I	L
K	W	H	Y	L	V	I	O	B	R	O	Z	J	T	S

Answers 47-49

PUZZLE 47

3	5	2	1	1	4
6	2	4	6	1	4
6	1	4	5	2	3
2	1	5	5	3	4
2	3	4	6	3	1

PUZZLE 48

W	S	K	G	J	E	D	E	A	B	E
X	M	J	L	F	A	G	C	B	C	F
Z	J	I	K	H	B	D	N	C	K	D
L	K	L	H	G	M	E	M	R	D	O
M	L	N	I	H	F	L	F	K	B	E
T	M	O	T	C	G	O	C	G	F	K
N	R	Q	E	H	D	N	A	H	B	G
M	O	R	F	T	X	M	F	J	K	J
Q	P	S	R	S	T	U	V	W	A	M
R	S	Q	S	K	T	H	M	D	K	O
T	T	W	R	X	M	U	L	T	Q	R
R	U	Y	Y	Q	V	G	V	S	T	W
V	W	T	X	W	X	W	Y	W	X	Y
Y	Z	Y	S	X	Y	D	A	Y	S	T

PUZZLE 49

		T	R	A	I	N		
			B	U	S			
				S	L	E	D	
	B	O	A	T				
		C	A	R				
			W	A	L	K		
A	I	R	P	L	A	N	E	
			B	I	K	E		
		T	R	A	C	T	O	R

Answers 50-53

PUZZLE 50

A

3	5	2	1	4
1	4	5	3	2
2	1	3	4	5
4	2	1	5	3
5	3	4	2	1

B

4	1	5	3	2
5	3	2	4	1
1	2	4	5	3
3	4	1	2	5
2	5	3	1	4

PUZZLE 51

The passcode is 385.

PUZZLE 52

A 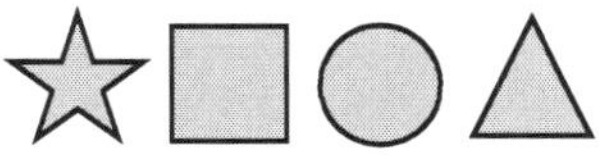

B 

PUZZLE 53

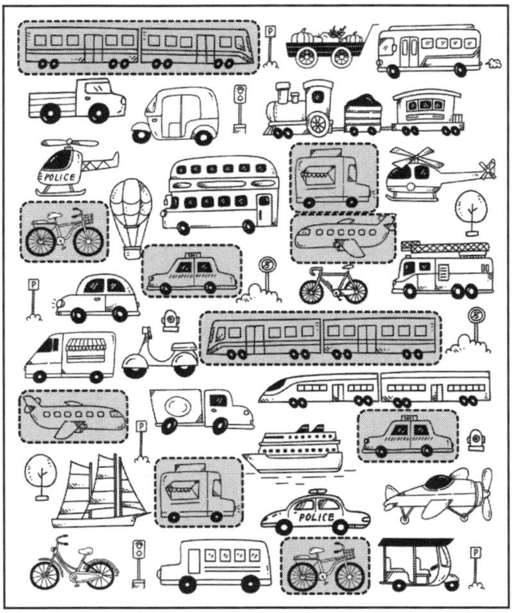

PUZZLE 54

2	1	5	7	4	6	9	3	8
6	9	4	3	8	2	5	7	1
8	3	7	5	1	9	2	4	6
3	4	2	6	5	8	1	9	7
5	6	8	1	9	7	3	2	4
1	7	9	2	3	4	6	8	5
9	8	1	4	2	5	7	6	3
7	2	3	8	6	1	4	5	9
4	5	6	9	7	3	8	1	2

PUZZLE 55

D is travelling to Scotland.
C has a black suitcase.

		Passenger				Destination			
		A	B	C	D	France	Mexico	Canada	Scotland
Suitcase	Pink	✗	✗	✗	✓	✗	✗	✗	✓
	Black	✗	✗	✓	✗	✗	✗	✓	✗
	Red	✓	✗	✗	✗	✓	✗	✗	✗
	Blue	✗	✓	✗	✗	✗	✓	✗	✗
Destination	France	✓	✗	✗	✗				
	Mexico	✗	✓	✗	✗				
	Canada	✗	✗	✓	✗				
	Scotland	✗	✗	✗	✓				

PUZZLE 56

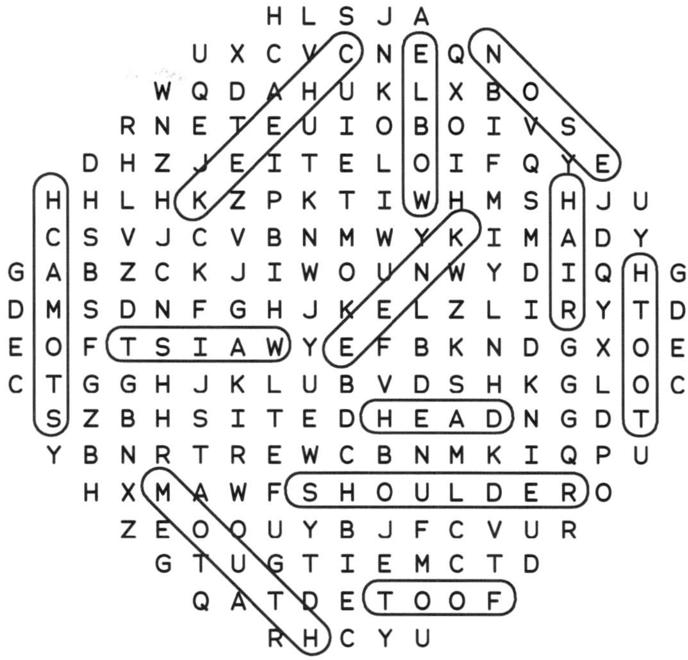

PUZZLE 57

PUZZLE 58

A 

B 

C 

D 

E 

PUZZLE 59

		F				R	A	I	N
C		O				A			
L	I	G	H	T	N	I	N	G	
O				H		N			
U				U		B		W	
D		S	U	N		O		I	
		T		D		W	I	N	D
S	H	O	W	E	R			T	
N		R		R				E	
O		M				W	A	R	M
W									

PUZZLE 60

6	4	2	2	2	1
6	3	1	5	5	1
5	4	1	2	6	3
5	6	2	3	1	2
1	6	4	1	5	2

PUZZLE 61

PUZZLE 62

The items on the list are:

1. scarf
2. earmuffs
3. socks
4. sweater
5. gloves
6. mittens
7. boots
8. jackets

PUZZLE 63

M	O	S	T	L	Y	S
U	N	N	Y	W	I	T
H	A	G	E	N	T	L
E	B	R	E	E	Z	E

Mostly sunny with a gentle breeze.

PUZZLE 64

A

2	4	1	3	5
1	2	5	4	3
4	5	3	2	1
5	3	4	1	2
3	1	2	5	4

B

1	3	2	5	4
5	2	4	3	1
3	4	5	1	2
2	1	3	4	5
4	5	1	2	3

PUZZLE 65

Abbie - Winter
Ben - Spring
Chloe - Autumn
David - Summer

Answers 66-69

PUZZLE 66

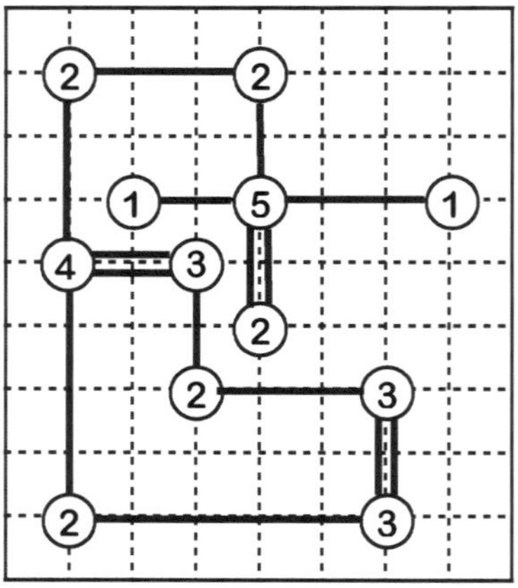

PUZZLE 67

163
73 90
31 42 48
13 18 24 24
6 7 11 13 11
2 4 3 8 5 6

PUZZLE 68

Route **B** goes to ice cream.

PUZZLE 69

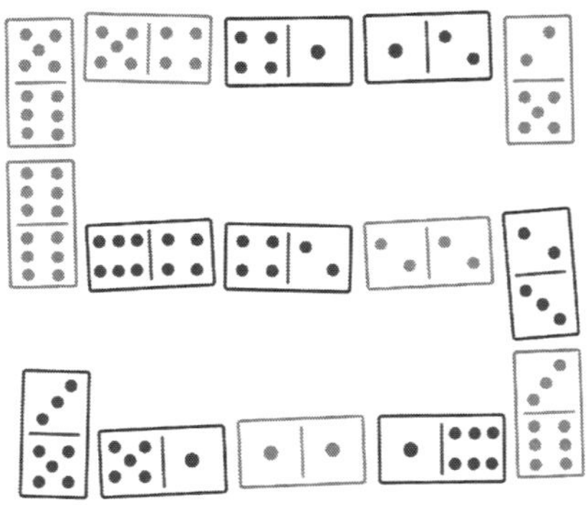

PUZZLE 70

9	1	6	7	7	2
9	5	1	8	2	6
1	5	2	3	3	7
6	2	6	5	6	3
7	9	4	6	7	9
7	6	9	5	3	7

PUZZLE 71

D

PUZZLE 72

The passcode is 756.

PUZZLE 73

The treasure is hidden in the map square of C and H.

PUZZLE 74

6	3	2	4	9	8	7	5	1
4	8	5	7	3	1	6	9	2
7	9	1	6	2	5	4	8	3
9	2	7	8	1	3	5	4	6
8	6	3	5	4	2	9	1	7
1	5	4	9	7	6	2	3	8
5	7	6	1	8	4	3	2	9
2	1	9	3	5	7	8	6	4
3	4	8	2	6	9	1	7	5

Answers 75-77

PUZZLE 75

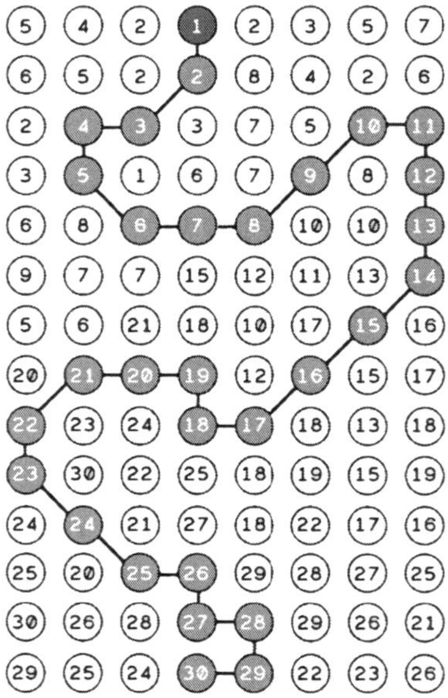

PUZZLE 76

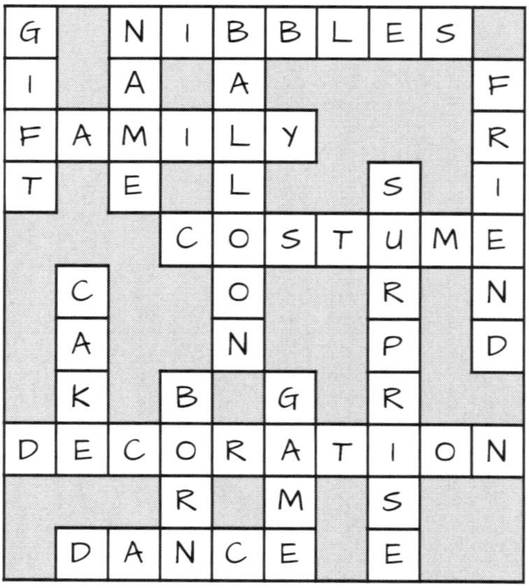

PUZZLE 77

A 

B 

PUZZLE 78

PUZZLE 79

An area with lots of trees	F		E	A	R
P	O	T	A	T	O
What chips and french fries are made of	R	To pull along	T	O	W
P	E	N	What we need to do when we're hungry	M	Use oars to move a boat / Excuse ___ !
One of many on a zebra	S	Greetings!	H	The smallest component of an element	M
S	T	R	I	P	E

PUZZLE 80

A

2		4		3	1
v		v			
1		3	>	2	4
3		1		4	2
4		2	>	1	3

B

3		4	1	2
1		3	2	4
2	>	1	4	3
				v
4		2	3	1

Answers 81-83

PUZZLE 81

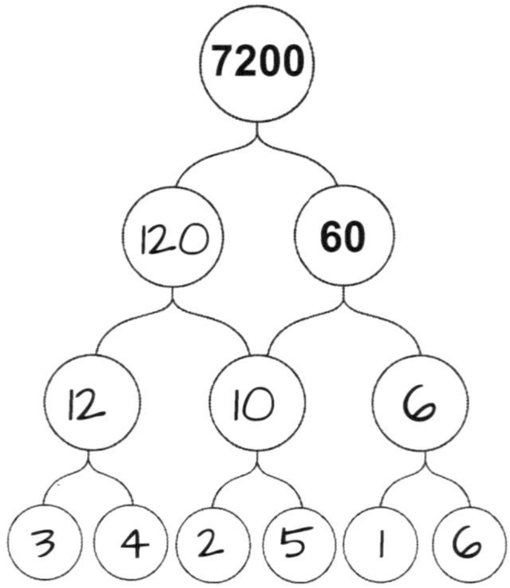

PUZZLE 82

5	2	1	6	7		8	8	4	5	2	3	
4				3			6	4	1			4
9			7	1	4	5	0	9	5			3
0	4	8		2	3	2	8	0		3	2	9
			0	6	8	7			9	3	6	
3	9	9	5	9	4		2		1	5	2	1
4			2		3	7	0	5	7			0
8	9	7	1	5		2	3	0		6	2	8
		1			5	8	6	3		8		9
3	1	8	0		0	0	2	4		9	3	2
7		6	9	4	1	2		3		3		
1	3	5	7					9	6	2	3	5

PUZZLE 83

PUZZLE 84

6	3	6	6	2	1
4	1	2	5	2	1
6	2	6	6	4	2
3	2	3	5	4	1
6	1	5	5	1	4

PUZZLE 85

```
L B H N J N E C K O K B L J G J N I M X
I A P Z I N L R E Y U I O E T U L F H C
G N J N E A K N D W E D C D F V D G D Y
D J D R R R F T G U I T A R U H H I J C
D O I I M C B G Z S V D H C I V C A C U
D H N J K L V U Y H N B G T R F V C R E
D E U D H U I G D G D G D R V B A C U P
T C H Q T N O E U F D D Z U D F C D H E
G H D F Y D L T U K H T H M F V I G D Y
E F S S M S I G D R U A Q P A Z N T Y X
D R U M D S N W E R D L H E B V O X S F
H B J N K W E K M D D F E T F V M F D Y
F R T V G O G N C N C N Q L U J R I T Z
L O F J L F H D F S S F H F E J A L F H
G H D L R N O I D R O C C A F V H G D Y
N C E T G U L K U C C U Y U F F U Y U J
G C G H J K K M O L I P T R I A N G L E
S W Q A Z W S X E D C V F R T G B N H Y
P I A N O I U L B G T F C D E R F H H Y
J K I J U J J H Y G T F V C D E A B U T
```

PUZZLE 86

A

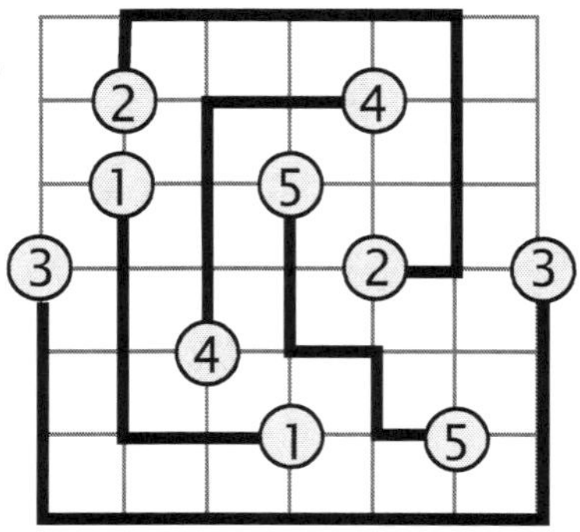

B

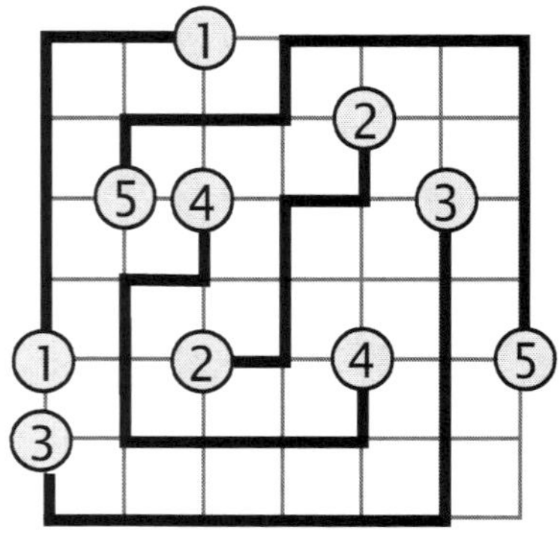

PUZZLE 87

The password is TEA359.

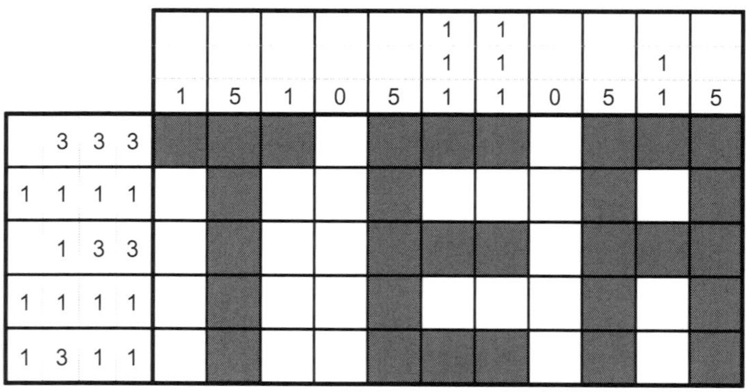

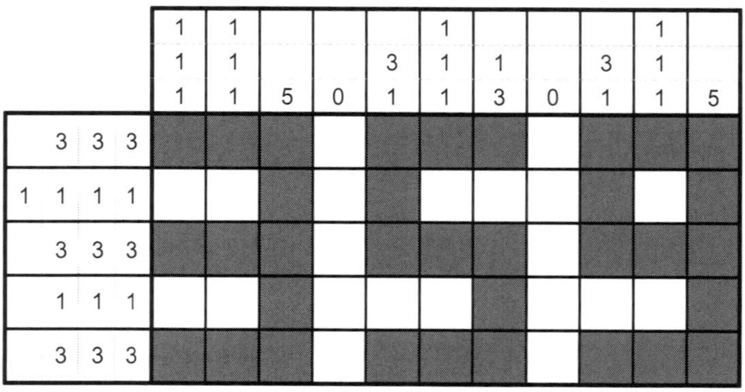

PUZZLE 88

B

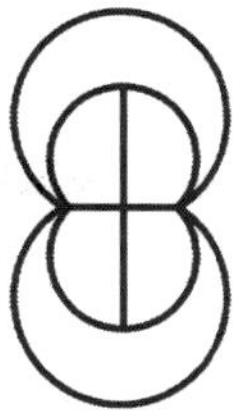

PUZZLE 89

PUZZLE 90

Answers 91-93

PUZZLE 91

PUZZLE 92

The items on the shopping list are:

1. bread
2. carrot
3. sausage
4. pizza
5. juice
6. apple
7. cupcake
8. tomato
9. banana
10. watermelon

PUZZLE 93

Ben is 9 and does swimming.
Adam is 10 and does cycling.
Daisy is 11 and does basketball.
Charlie is 12 and does tennis.

		Child			
		Ben	Adam	Daisy	Charlie
Age	12	✗	✗	✗	✓
	9	✓	✗	✗	✗
	10	✗	✓	✗	✗
	11	✗	✗	✓	✗
Sport	Basketball	✗	✗	✓	✗
	Tennis	✗	✗	✗	✓
	Swimming	✓	✗	✗	✗
	Cycling	✗	✓	✗	✗

PUZZLE 94

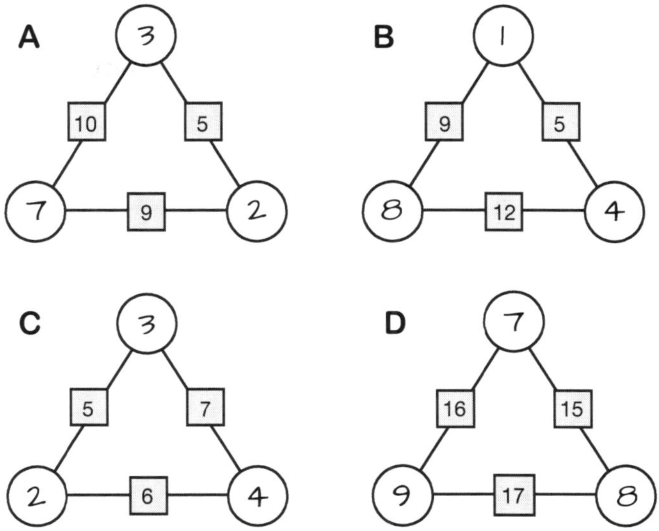

PUZZLE 95

8	6	5	7	9	2	3	4	1
7	4	3	8	5	1	2	6	9
9	2	1	6	3	4	8	7	5
5	3	4	2	1	6	9	8	7
1	9	8	3	4	7	5	2	6
6	7	2	9	8	5	1	3	4
4	8	7	5	2	9	6	1	3
2	1	9	4	6	3	7	5	8
3	5	6	1	7	8	4	9	2

PUZZLE 96 The passcode is 6704.

Answers 97-99

PUZZLE 97

		G	N	O	M	E			
		W	E	R	E	W	O	L	F
				D	R	A	G	O	N
			V	A	M	P	I	R	E
				F	A	I	R	Y	
			U	N	I	C	O	R	N
W	I	Z	A	R	D				

PUZZLE 98

8	3	7		6	4	1	0		8	7	3	1
9				8		2		1	7	4	3	
0	4	5	6	7		5		0	6	5	8	
4		2		2	5	8	4	3		5	8	0
2	3	3			5		6	8	0	4		0
	3		8		8		7					6
0	4	1	4	5		6	3	7		5	5	4
	6		9				9		1	3	7	9
		1	8	2	9	6	0		2	2	6	
	3	8	3	5				3	9	6	8	3
2	9	6		7				3		6		0
	6	5	3	7	9		8	4	4	3	8	1

PUZZLE 99

Dad was born in 1972, the year of the Rat.
Mum was born in 1978, the year of the Horse.
Daughter was born in 2010, the year of the Tiger.
Son was born in 2015, the year of the Goat.

Answers 100-101

PUZZLE 100

4	4	**9**	7	6	9
6	5	3	6	**4**	5
5	**1**	6	8	**3**	7
9	**7**	5	6	8	**2**
6	9	4	**8**	6	9
4	3	1	7	5	**6**

PUZZLE 101

PUZZLE 102

PUZZLE 103

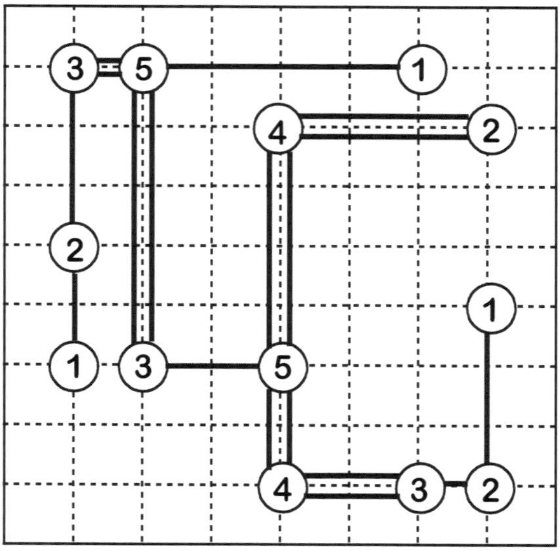

Printed in Great Britain
by Amazon

83295867R00082